BOOK TWO

# BIOLOGY FOR YOU

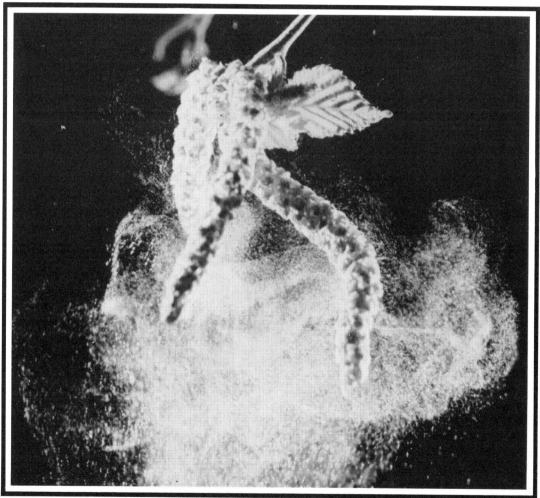

# Clare Smallman

## Hutchinson

London Melbourne Sydney Auckland Johannesburg

# Contents

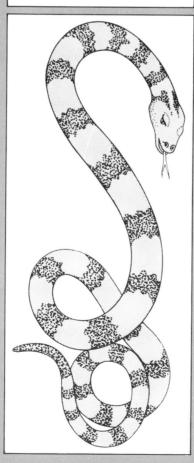

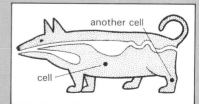

another cell

cell

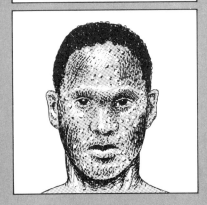

Hutchinson & Co. (Publishers) Ltd

An imprint of the Hutchinson Publishing Group

17-21 Conway Street, London W1P 6JD

Hutchinson Group (Australia) Pty Ltd
30-32 Cremorne Street, Richmond South, Victoria 3121
PO Box 151, Broadway, New South Wales 2007

Hutchinson Group (NZ) Ltd
32-34 View Road, PO Box 40-086, Glenfield, Auckland 10

Hutchinson Group (SA) (Pty) Ltd
PO Box 337, Bergvlei 2012, South Africa

© Clare Smallman 1983
Illustrations © Hutchinson & Co. (Publishers) Ltd

Illustrations by John Brennan, Ray and Corinne Burrows

Printed in Great Britain by The Anchor Press Ltd and bound by Wm Brendon & Son Ltd both of Tiptree, Essex

**British Library Cataloguing in Publication Data**
Smallman, Clare
   Biology for you.
   2
   1. Biology
   I. Title
   574      QH308.7
ISBN 0 09 1411319

**Acknowledgements**
Photographs reproduced by permission of Biophoto Associates p 28;   Mary Evans Picture Library pp 112, 122;   E. G. Mercer p 18;   Terry Williams p 115;   Trustees of the British Museum p 75.   Thanks are due to the following examination boards for permission to reproduce past examination questions: Associated Lancashire Schools Examining Board; East Anglian Examinations Board; East Midland Regional Examinations Board; London Regional Examining Board; North West Regional Examinations Board; South-East Regional Examinations Board; Southern Regional Examinations Board; South Western Examinations Board; Welsh Joint Education Committee; West Midlands Examination Board; West Yorkshire and Lindsey Regional Examining Board.

For Mark, Juliet and James

# Why move?

It's obvious why things move – or is it? Make your own list to check below. (Hint: **moving** is any change in position; **locomotion** is a change in place.)

the plant moves its leaves towards the light

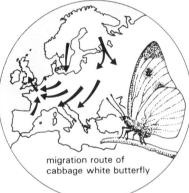

the frog moves its tongue to catch the fly

Here are some of the reasons:

1. Organisms move to collect the raw materials they need to live – such as sunlight and food.

2. They move to get out of problem situations – such as being eaten, or poor weather, or climate changes.

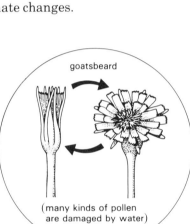

goatsbeard

(many kinds of pollen are damaged by water)

migration route of cabbage white butterfly

3. They move to avoid overcrowding.

4. And they move for sex.

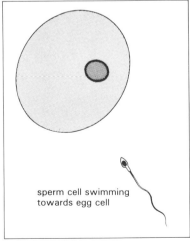

sperm cell swimming towards egg cell

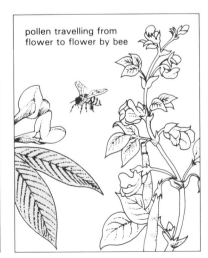

pollen travelling from flower to flower by bee

Some organisims 'hitch' lifts to save energy – examples include pollen, some seeds, and gliders.

flying squirrels are really gliders

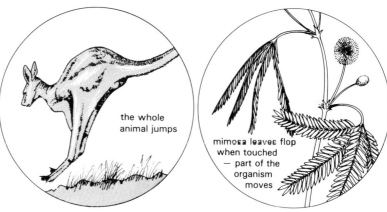
the whole animal jumps

mimosa leaves flop when touched – part of the organism moves

Many organisms are self-propelled – using lots of energy in the process.

Movement can involve the whole of an organism, or just a part.

Organisms need mechanisms
(a) for movement
(b) for working out where they are going and how far they have got – **sensing changes** – and
(c) for making sure everything works together when it is supposed to – **co-ordination.**

a co-ordination system – brain and nerves

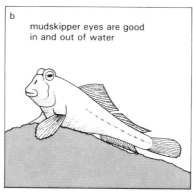
b
mudskipper eyes are good in and out of water

They need an energy supply too – remember *Biology for You 1*.

All this includes green plants, which manage to combine some of their moving with growing.

The first part of this book is about movement and all that goes with it – the rest is not unconnected with sex.

# Dispersal- the hitch-hikers

Organisms need space, for growth and for collecting raw materials such as water. Once they have grown roots, plants are stuck in one spot – it is their seeds that travel. This spreading out is known as **dispersal**. Any part of a plant which is dispersed is called a **propagule**. Animals must disperse, too. They can usually move themselves, perhaps in different ways at different stages in their lives. Some, like seeds, rely on help. How do they manage?

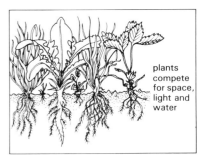

plants compete for space, light and water

The most popular way to hitch a lift is by **wind**.

Small seeds float away, and so do fungal spores and bacteria. All these propagules are light. Heavier ones may have **wings** or **parachutes**.

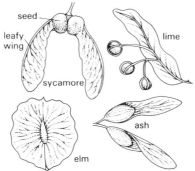

seed
leafy wing
sycamore
lime
ash
elm

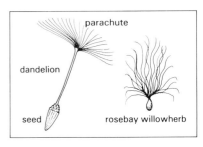

parachute
dandelion
seed
rosebay willowherb

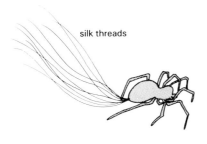

silk threads

Both parachutes and wings catch the wind and hold the seed in the air longer. Some small animals use the same trick. Money spiders 'balloon' from place to place on silk threads, and aphids ride wind currents from plant to plant.

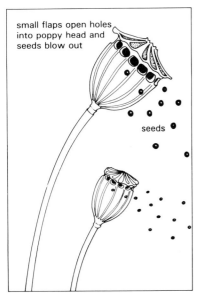

small flaps open holes into poppy head and seeds blow out

seeds

Some plants help themselves. Poppy heads dry out and sway in the wind. The seeds fall out through small holes which open when the weather is dry.

More excitingly – some plants catapult their seeds away from them. Geraniums do this. The fruit dries and twists suddenly, flinging the seeds out. The wind helps, too.

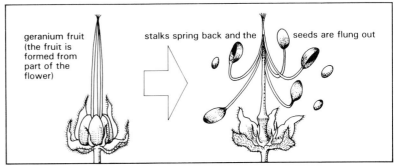

geranium fruit (the fruit is formed from part of the flower)

stalks spring back and the seeds are flung out

Seeds can be carried by **animals**, often when the fruit is eaten. The seed may be dropped – like an apple whose core you throw into a hedge – or it may be eaten as well. Then the seed travels through the gut and out the other end – along with instant manure. Some 'stones' have to be partly digested before the seeds inside can begin to grow out.

Animals which store seeds for food and forget them also help in dispersal. Squirrels are an example.

And of course there are seeds with hooks – the ones that really do hitch lifts on an animal's fur, a bird's legs and your trousers.

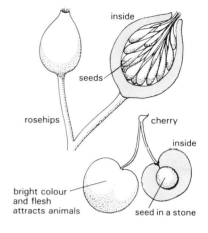

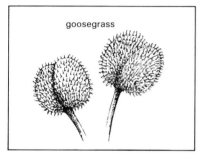

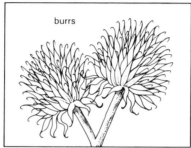

Some small insects use the same trick.

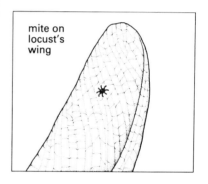

Lastly, some things are dispersed by **water**.

Life started in water. Seaweeds and other water plants rely on water currents to disperse them. So do many small water animals.

Island plants often travel to other islands by water. Coconuts have a hairy husk which helps them float. They are not damaged by salt water – they travel all over the world. They may also carry small animals like ants with them.

# Single cells and movement

Single cells, on their own or as part of a larger organism, have two (or three) ways of moving – unless they just drift.

**Cytoplasmic movements**
These keep the contents of plant cells moving. In some cells, the cytoplasm can be seen streaming around the edges. This helps mix up materials in the cell. Some people think threads of cytoplasm connect cells, and things like sugars can be passed from cell to cell in this way.

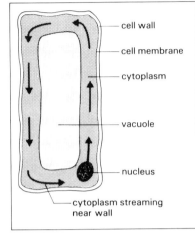

cell wall
cell membrane
cytoplasm
vacuole
nucleus
cytoplasm streaming near wall

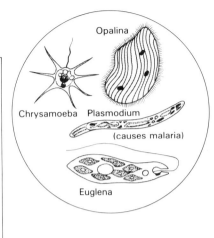

Opalina
Chrysamoeba   Plasmodium
(causes malaria)
Euglena

Cytoplasmic streaming can move cells from place to place. White blood cells and animals like Amoeba travel this way. They live in liquids (water, blood and so on) but usually move on a surface.

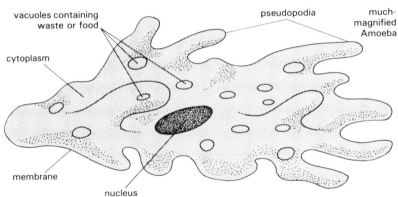

vacuoles containing waste or food
pseudopodia
much-magnified Amoeba
cytoplasm
membrane
nucleus

The large projections are called **pseudopodia**. They are important in moving and in trapping food. Pseudopodia are temporary – always being formed and then disappearing. They are produced by cytoplasmic streaming.

These cells seem to change their cytoplasm from being jelly-like to being quite runny. The runny and jelly parts move against each other to move the cell. This uses up energy. It is not certain exactly how Amoeba and white blood cells move.

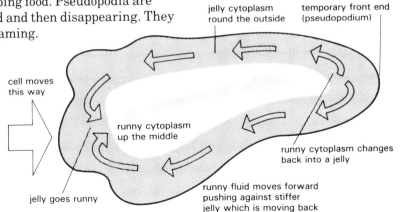

jelly cytoplasm round the outside
temporary front end (pseudopodium)
cell moves this way
runny cytoplasm up the middle
runny cytoplasm changes back into a jelly
jelly goes runny
runny fluid moves forward pushing against stiffer jelly which is moving back

## Flagella and cilia – the moving threads

These are thread-like and they beat against the liquid around them, pushing or pulling the cell along. They allow cells to move freely in liquids like water and blood. They differ in size and numbers.

**Flagella** come in ones and twos, and are long compared to their cell.

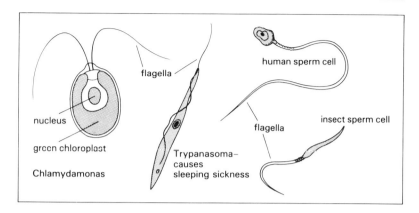

The shape of the flagella is different in the power (pushing) stroke and in the recovery stroke – think of doing the breast stroke.

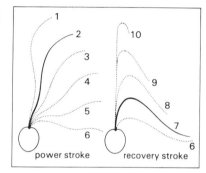

**Cilia** are smaller and are found in large groups. They beat in rhythm, and in action look like a field of grass rippling in the wind.

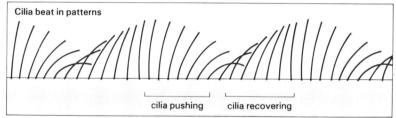

Cilia beat in patterns

cilia pushing     cilia recovering

Single celled organisms like Paramecium have cilia for moving and food collecting. Larger organisms find other uses for cilia. The cells lining the air passage in your lungs use cilia to help remove particles of dirt.

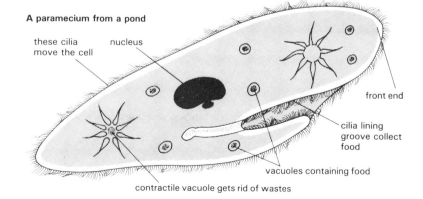

A paramecium from a pond

PS: You'd need a microscope to see all these cells. The magnification varies from drawing to drawing.

# Muscles and soft bodied animals

Larger animals rely on muscles for movement. Muscles use up energy when they **contract** – become short and fat – and pull against something. For soft-bodied animals that something is water.

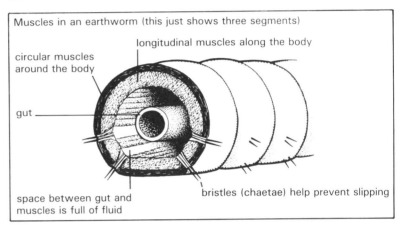

Sea anemone (an animal) muscles in the tentacles help hold small animals for food

circular muscles form a ring

longitudinal muscles run up and down

circular muscles contracted

longitudinal muscles contracted

In most movements two sets of muscles are needed, one to do and one to undo. They act in turn. When one set is contracted, the other **relaxes** – allows itself to be pulled out long and thin again. Such alternating muscles are called **antagonistic muscles**. Pairs of antagonistic muscles move animals like the earthworm. In this case the water they push against is inside the animal.

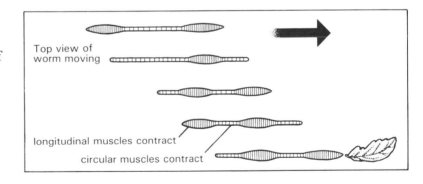

Muscles in an earthworm (this just shows three segments)

longitudinal muscles along the body

circular muscles around the body

gut

space between gut and muscles is full of fluid

bristles (chaetae) help prevent slipping

The circular and longitudinal muscles take it in turns to contract and make a pattern of waves down the worm's body.

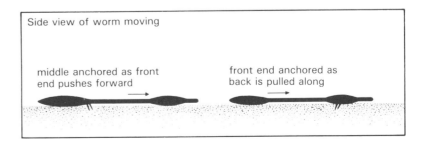

Top view of worm moving

longitudinal muscles contract

circular muscles contract

The bristles anchor different parts of the worm as needed.

Side view of worm moving

middle anchored as front end pushes forward

front end anchored as back is pulled along

# Summary and questions

## Summary

All living things move – that is, change their position in some way. Dispersal involves moving to new places to prevent overcrowding. Many organisms move themselves; others (especially the seed plants) take advantage of wind, water and animal movements. Active movement comes in many forms. Single cells move either as the result of the beating of hair like flagella or cilia, or by cytoplasmic movement. Many-celled animals use muscles which contract and pull against something – body fluids in the case of worms. Paired muscles contract and relax in turn to produce complete movements and are known as antagonistic muscles.

## Questions

1. Write out the whole paragraph below, filling in the spaces.

   Moving from place to place is also called _____. Movement also includes changes in position – for example, plant leaves turning in order to catch as much _____ as possible. Other reasons for moving include finding a mate, avoiding _____, finding _____ and escaping from _____. Most organisms use up _____ in moving, but some are carried from place to place by wind, _____ or _____. This is often true in the dispersal of _____, but it is also the way some small animals travel.

2. Explain what is meant by the following – and give an example in each case:
   (a) dispersal
   (b) propagule
   (c) antagonistic muscles
   (d) cytoplasmic streaming
   (e) pseudopodium

3. Draw and label
   (a) Amoeba
   (b) Paramecium
   (c) a section through an earthworm
   What is the big difference (in your opinion) between the movement of the earthworm and movement in Amoeba and Paramecium?

4. Leeches are soft-bodied animals which can move by looping (see right). They have circular and longitudinal muscles which act antagonistically in their body wall. Which are contracted in A and which in C?

5. Draw and add two labels (as well as the name) to
   (a) a seed dispersed by wind
   (b) a seed dispersed by animals
   (c) a self-propelled seed
   (d) an animal dispersed by wind
   Explain why these kinds of dispersal are so important to green plants. Write at least four sentences.

6. From the pages on single cells and movement, name
   (a) one cell you're sure is a plant, and say why (don't use the plant cell diagram for cytoplasmic movement)
   (b) two single cell organisms (not parts of organisms) moved by flagella
   (c) one organism in which cytoplasmic movement is important. How does cytoplasmic streaming work (as far as we know)?
   (d) two organisms which move by cilia. Explain how cilia work – diagrams may help. What can they be used for besides locomotion?

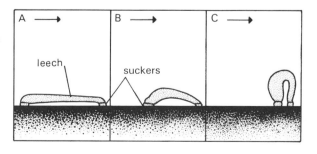

# Muscles and bones

**Vertebrates** – animals with bones – have something solid for muscles to pull on. Here are a pair of antagonistic muscles in the human arm. The **biceps** flexes the lower arm – pulls it up – when it contracts. The **triceps** extends or straightens the arm. Try it.

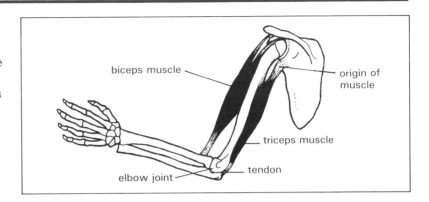

biceps muscle

origin of muscle

triceps muscle

tendon

elbow joint

Like many muscles, the triceps and biceps are attached to bone by **tendons**.

Muscles (meat) are red. They have a good blood supply – they do a lot of work. Tendons are white, tough and non-stretchy. Live bone is pinkish – there's a lot going on inside (including making red blood cells).

There are two main kinds of muscle cell.

muscle

tendon

bone

ridge of bone where tendon is attached

Striated muscle

long muscle cells with many nuclei

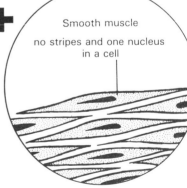

Smooth muscle

no stripes and one nucleus in a cell

**Striated** muscle has long muscle cells with many nuclei. It looks stripey under a microscope. It's the muscle you can choose to use – or not.

**Smooth** muscle has no stripes and one nucleus in each cell. This kind of muscle is found in the walls of guts, blood vessels and the uterus – you don't consciously control it.

Both kinds of muscle use lots of energy and have a good blood supply. They are also carefully controlled – even if you're not aware of it. It hurts when things go wrong. Tetanus happens when all the muscles of the body contract together. It is caused by a toxin (poison) made by a bacterium. It's not only painful – both sets of breathing muscles cancel each other, so you can't breathe. Other systems also fail and you die. Could anti-tetanus jabs be a good idea?

Muscles and bones act as a lever system – what they can do depends on the kind of lever. Try them out to check the effect.

This type has a pivot (turning point) between the load being moved and the effort, which can be a push or a pull. This set-up makes it easier to move a weight. (This is type 1.)

effort (push)

lever (use a ruler)

pivot (anything the ruler will balance on)    load

So does this – these levers magnify effort (type 2).

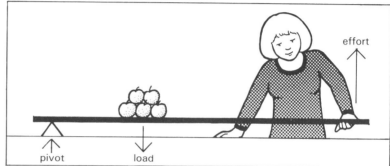

effort

pivot    load

This one is a little different – the effort is between load and pivot. It's harder to move the load – but it moves further. This set-up magnifies distance (type 3).

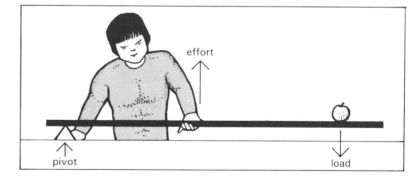

effort

pivot    load

Watch out for levers doing different jobs in the body. The arm magnifies distance (the elbow joint is the pivot).

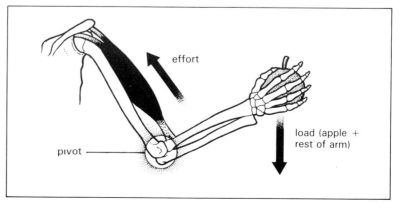

effort

load (apple + rest of arm)

pivot

All is well as long as bones don't bend, joints don't seize up, and your muscles can provide enough pull.

15

# Bones and joints

Bone is strong and light. **Strength** comes from the material and from the way it is arranged. Bone is made of calcium salts held together by fibres of collagen (a protein). **Lightness** comes from using as little solid bone as possible.

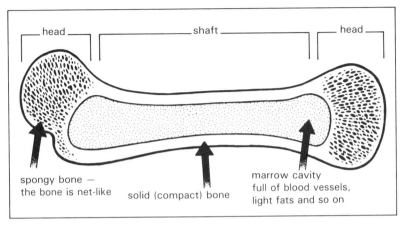

head _____ shaft _____ head

spongy bone — the bone is net-like

solid (compact) bone

marrow cavity full of blood vessels, light fats and so on

Short bones may be a thin shell of solid bone around spongy bone. Saw a vertebra in half and see.

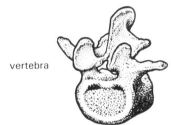

vertebra

Even solid bone isn't solid. Running through it are blood vessels surrounded by bone-making cells. Bones need constant repair. If bone cells die, as they do as people get older, bones become brittle.

**Bones grow**, often from cartilage-like pre-bones. **Cartilage** proper is found in the ear and end of the nose. It is quite flexible (it has no calcium salts). In bones, cartilage is gradually replaced by bone – starting in the middle of the shaft.

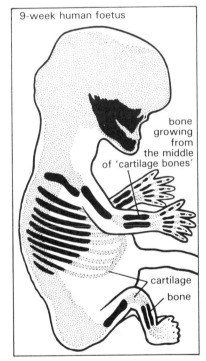

9-week human foetus

bone growing from the middle of 'cartilage bones'

cartilage

bone

Bone doesn't stretch. For a marrow cavity to grow, bone must grow on the outside while material is removed from the inside.

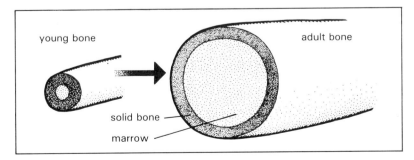

young bone

adult bone

solid bone

marrow

**Joints** happen where bones meet. They are often made to allow movement. The basic synovial or moveable joint looks like this.

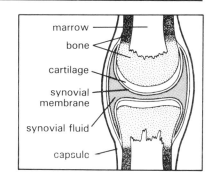

**Cartilage** provides a smooth surface with a bit of give.
**Synovial membrane** lines the joint. It makes synovial fluid.
**Synovial fluid** fills the small space between the bone heads. It acts as a lubricant and reduces friction.
**Capsule** helps hold the joint together. There are also ligaments (not shown) doing this job.

Joints move in various ways. The simplest movement is gliding, where one bone slides across another. Gliding joints are found between some of the bones of the hands and feet. In other joints, movement may be more complicated. Here are four other types of joint.

**Cartilagenous joints**
These allow a limited amount of movement. They are not synovial joints.

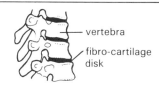

Example: between the vertebrae, where disks act as shock absorbers.

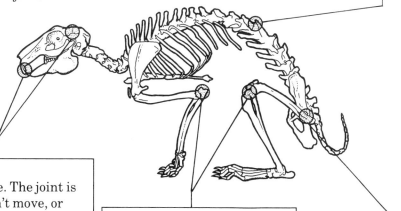

**Fixed joints**
Bone meets bone. The joint is strong but doesn't move, or only gives a little. These aren't synovial joints.

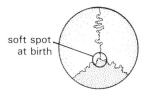

(Skull bones are not quite fixed at birth, to allow easier delivery.)
Examples: bones of skull, teeth in jaw.

**Hinge joints**
Bones fit neatly together and act like a door hinge. The joint moves backwards and forwards but not sideways.

Examples: joints between finger bones, knee joint.

**Ball and socket joints**
The joint allows a lot of movement – this type is most likely to dislocate.

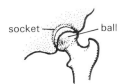

Examples: hip and shoulder joints.

# The human skeleton

The skeleton is a collection of bones which supports soft organs like the guts; protects delicate ones like lungs, brain and kidneys; and provides something for muscles to pull on.

X-rays show up bone structure. They can go through soft tissues but not through the calcium salts in bones.

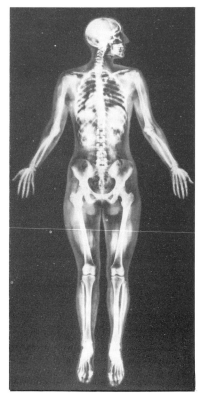

**Male skeleton**

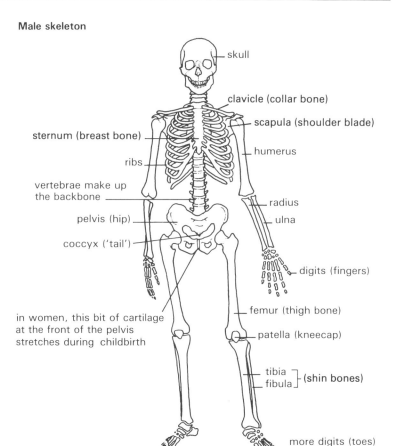

skull

clavicle (collar bone)

scapula (shoulder blade)

sternum (breast bone)

humerus

ribs

vertebrae make up the backbone

radius

ulna

pelvis (hip)

coccyx ('tail')

digits (fingers)

in women, this bit of cartilage at the front of the pelvis stretches during childbirth

femur (thigh bone)

patella (kneecap)

tibia
fibula } (shin bones)

more digits (toes)

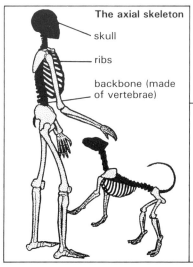

**The axial skeleton**

skull

ribs

backbone (made of vertebrae)

The bones of the skeleton can be divided into two groups: the **axial** skeleton, based on the backbone, and the **appendages**.

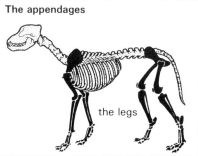

**The appendages**

the legs

18

# Summary and questions

## Summary

In vertebrates, the body is supported and protected by bones (plus cartilage). They are arranged as a skeleton, made up of an axial skeleton plus appendages. Bones are strong and light. Muscles move the body by pulling on the bones, which act as levers. Joints – where bones move against each other – are designed for strength and reducing friction. There are three main kinds of joint: fixed, cartilagenous and synovial joints. Synovial joints include gliding joints, ball and socket joints and hinge joints. Each of these allows a different kind of movement.

## Questions

1. Consider the following muscles and bones:

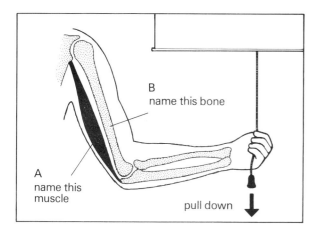

B name this bone

A name this muscle

pull down

   (a) Name muscle A.
   (b) Name bone B.
   (c) Does this lever magnify distance or effort?

2. Explain the difference between each of these pairs:
   (a) the biceps and triceps
   (b) solid (compact) bone and spongy bone
   (c) bone and cartilage
   (d) the axial skeleton and appendages
   (e) smooth and striated muscles

3. (a) Draw a hinge joint. Give two examples of this kind of joint.
   (b) Draw a ball and socket joint. Give two examples of this kind of joint.
   (c) Draw a diagram to show how a muscle is attached to a bone.

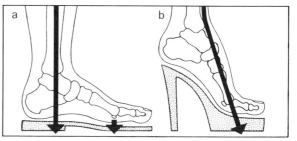

a b

4. The diagrams show which bones take the body mass when different kinds of shoe are worn. It is often said that very high heels cause foot troubles – do the diagrams support this idea? Explain your answer.

5. Explain why each of these is true:
   (a) Synovial fluid is important for easy movement.
   (b) Bones like vertebrae have large projections sticking out.
   (c) There is a lot of space inside bones.
   (d) The skull bones of new born babies haven't completely fused (stuck together). They can still slide a bit.
   (e) Diseases like arthritis and osteoarthritis are very painful.
   (f) X-rays show up bones.

6. In question 4 there was a diagram showing the bones of the foot. The foot is straightened when the calf muscle, which is attached to the heel bone, contracts. Decide for yourself where the pivot in your foot is, and draw a diagram to show how the foot acts as a lever. Do you think it magnifies distance (moves you further) or effort (makes it easy to move your body mass)?

# Walking and running

Legs keep the body off the ground.

Short splayed legs (attached on the sides) mean slow moving.

Legs placed under the body mean speed. It helps if they're long.

Once off the ground and on four legs an animal becomes rather like a bridge.

Slow

Fast

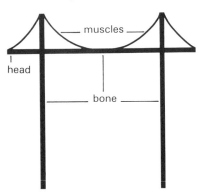

muscles

head

bone

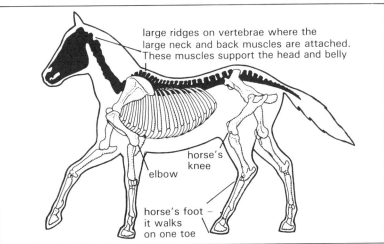

large ridges on vertebrae where the large neck and back muscles are attached. These muscles support the head and belly

horse's knee

elbow

horse's foot — it walks on one toe

Many small runners and jumpers have bendy backbones. The flexible spine means extra spring for extra speed. Rabbits and greyhounds are like this.

**Some speeds for short distances**
cheetah – 50 mph+
greyhound – 40 mph
racehorse – 40 mph
black mamba – 7 mph
(that's fast for a snake)

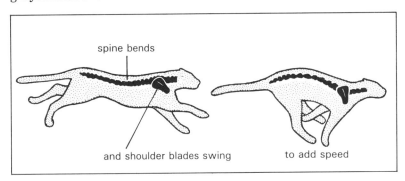

spine bends

and shoulder blades swing

to add speed

Larger and heavier animals like horses have a stiffer backbone – luckily for us. Their speed comes from long legs.

However, the larger you get, the easier it is to break your legs as you run – why?

One problem is that bones are bones – whatever size they are, the material is the same. A large animal like the elephant has enormously thick leg bones, and needs them.

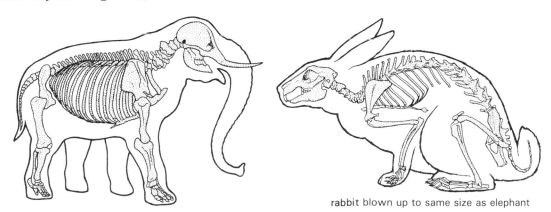

rabbit blown up to same size as elephant

A rabbit the size of an elephant would collapse – its bones would be crushed by its own weight. Body mass increases faster than leg size. The body mass of a large animal is more than its bones and muscles can support, unless it has extra thick bones like the elephant. (That's why *really* large animals – whales – live in the sea, where the water supports them.) An elephant's legs are strong enough for running but aren't springy enough for jumping. It's quite safe to keep elephants in zoos with only a ditch between them and the visitors.

extra curve near the bottom of the backbone in an adult

Man is one of the few animals to walk upright for much of his life. It's meant changes to muscles and bones, especially in the foot and back. Some changes are not complete, which is why people have hip and back trouble as they get older – and feet ache if they are badly treated. Changes in the pelvis mean birth is more difficult for humans than for other animals. Babies have to turn a corner to get out, instead of having a straightforward slide helped by gravity.

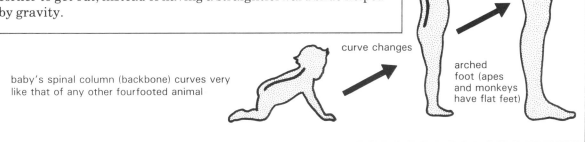

baby's spinal column (backbone) curves very like that of any other fourfooted animal

curve changes

arched foot (apes and monkeys have flat feet)

# Flying

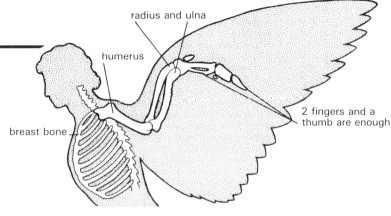

radius and ulna

humerus

breast bone

2 fingers and a thumb are enough

You've always wanted to fly? Well, you'll have to make some changes.

You'll need a **large surface** to push against the air. Bats use skin, birds have feathers. Either way your arm bones will have to change.

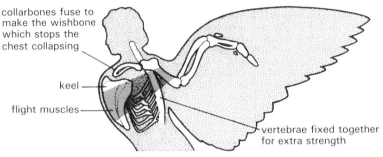

collarbones fuse to make the wishbone which stops the chest collapsing

keel

flight muscles

vertebrae fixed together for extra strength

You'll need **muscles** to move your flying surface. Birds have a large keel instead of a flat breast bone for attaching their flight (breast) muscles. You'll need a keel sticking out over a metre in front of you. At least a third of your weight will be flight muscles.

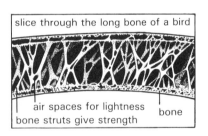

slice through the long bone of a bird

air spaces for lightness
bone struts give strength
bone

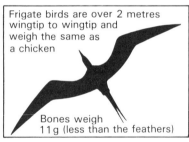

Frigate birds are over 2 metres wingtip to wingtip and weigh the same as a chicken

Bones weigh 11g (less than the feathers)

You'll have to **lose weight**. Birds have many hollow bones.

Ways of saving weight might include giving up half your sex organs, sweat glands and jaw. Birds do it. You could also get smaller. **Air spaces** are useful in breathing. Air sacs in them can open off the lungs and help gas exchange. A large heart helps. Flight muscles need a lot of fuel.

To avoid a nose-dive, reduce the size of your head. Some of your brain will have to go. The rule is: develop the bits you need for flying and shrink the rest.

You'll be warmer with feathers all over. Balancing is easier with tail feathers. Claws are better for landing than flat feet, and you'll need strong walking muscles, attached to your feet by long tendons.

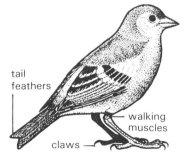

tail feathers

walking muscles

claws

## Flying

Learning to use the equipment takes practice. Flying involves keeping up and going forward. **Keeping up** is easy. The shape of the wing near the body does it – like an aeroplane wing.

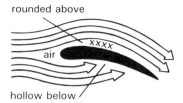

rounded above

xxxx

air

hollow below

Air going **over** the wing speeds up. The result is low pressure (at **xxxx**) which pulls the wing up. This is called lift.

**Going forward.** The wing-tips flick back and down much faster than the rest of the wing, and push the bird along.

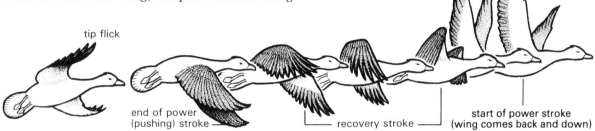

tip flick

end of power (pushing) stroke

recovery stroke

start of power stroke (wing comes back and down)

You'll have to decide in advance what kind of flying you want to do – slow or fast.

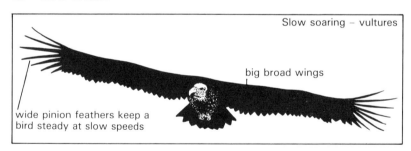

Slow soaring – vultures

big broad wings

wide pinion feathers keep a bird steady at slow speeds

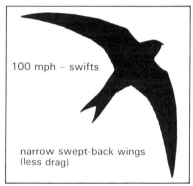

100 mph – swifts

narrow swept-back wings (less drag)

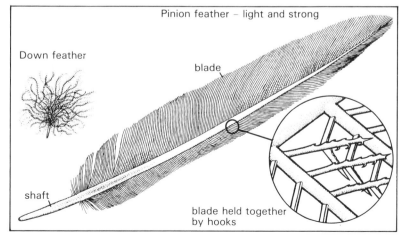

Pinion feather – light and strong

Down feather

blade

shaft

blade held together by hooks

There are pinion feathers, down feathers and several types in between. They are all made from much-changed skin cells.

# Swimming

Fish push water backwards – mainly with their tails – and end up moving forwards themselves.

tail and tail fin move most

The backbone acts as a chain of levers which can move from side to side. (In swimming mammals like whales the backbone moves up and down.) The final powerful flick of the tail is the end result of a wave of muscle contractions moving down the body.

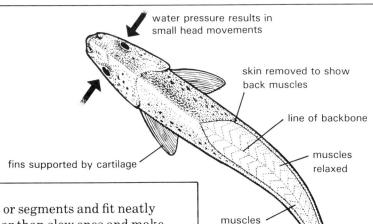

water pressure results in small head movements

skin removed to show back muscles

line of backbone

muscles relaxed

fins supported by cartilage

muscles contracted

tail

tail fin

The muscles are arranged in blocks or segments and fit neatly together. Fast fish are more muscular than slow ones and make better eating.

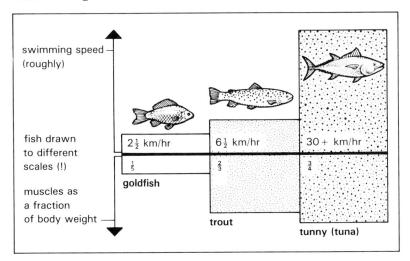

swimming speed (roughly)

fish drawn to different scales (!)

muscles as a fraction of body weight

| $2\frac{1}{2}$ km/hr | $6\frac{1}{2}$ km/hr | 30 + km/hr |
| --- | --- | --- |
| $\frac{1}{5}$ | $\frac{2}{3}$ | $\frac{3}{4}$ |
| **goldfish** | **trout** | **tunny (tuna)** |

Fast fish are also more streamlined. Water slows moving objects by swirling around them and by sticking to them (friction). The result is called drag. Ways of reducing drag vary with speed but a smooth outline helps – and smooth scales.

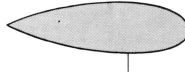

a streamlined shape

shape is widest at about $\frac{1}{3}$ length from the front

**Control** is the job of the fins, apart from the tail fins. The main brakes are the **pectoral fins**, with help from the **pelvic fins** in rapid halts. The pectoral fins alone might have an effect like stopping a bike suddenly using only the front brakes.

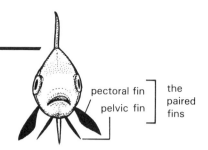

pectoral fin
pelvic fin
the paired fins

Rolling movements are also controlled by the paired fins – with help from the **anal** and **dorsal** fins, adjustable up-and-down fins. They act rather like a boat's keel, and also prevent side-to-side swings or yawing.

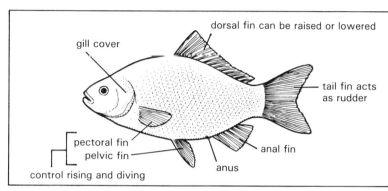

dorsal fin can be raised or lowered
gill cover
tail fin acts as rudder
pectoral fin
pelvic fin
control rising and diving
anus
anal fin

Fins can change their job and do the pushing in some fish. They can also be used for protection.

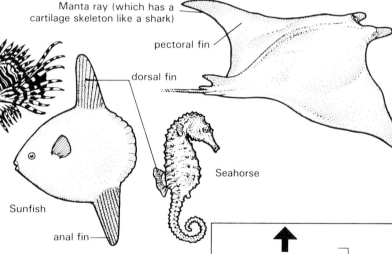

first 11 dorsal spines are poisonous

Dragon fish

the rest of the dorsal and pectoral fins are warnings

Manta ray (which has a cartilage skeleton like a shark)
pectoral fin
dorsal fin

Seahorse

Sunfish
anal fin

**Keeping up.** Muscle, bone and cartilage are heavier than water. Sharks, all cartilage and flesh, have to swim all the time or they sink. Bony fish (most of the ones you eat) have a float inside them – a **swim bladder** full of air (mostly oxygen) which opens off the gut.

Fish can control the amount of air in the swim bladder so that they balance exactly.

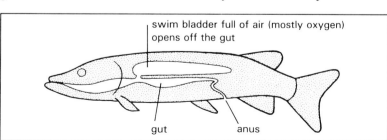

swim bladder full of air (mostly oxygen) opens off the gut

gut
anus

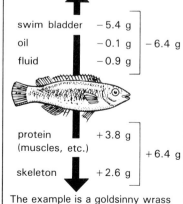

swim bladder    − 5.4 g
oil    − 0.1 g    − 6.4 g
fluid    − 0.9 g

protein (muscles, etc.)    + 3.8 g    + 6.4 g
skeleton    + 2.6 g

The example is a goldsinny wrass

# Summary and questions

## Summary

Organisms with backbones walk, run, fly and swim. They all have the same basic skeleton, but the shape and size of their bones depends upon their way of life. Large animals have large bones for strength, flyers have light hollow bones and so on. They all use muscles to move bone (or cartilage) 'levers' so that they push against something – the ground, air or water. Some animals are streamlined and muscled for speed, but many others do very well at slower speeds.

## Questions

1. Explain the difference between
   (a) pectoral and pelvic fins
   (b) anal and dorsal fins
   (c) paired fins and other fins
   (d) the spine movements of a whale and a trout
   (e) pinion and down feathers
   (f) the blade and shaft of a feather
   (g) the appendages of a fish and a bird

2. Say whether (and why) you would expect
   (a) manta rays to have swim bladders
   (b) dragon fish to be fast swimmers
   (c) frigate birds to fly slowly easily
   (d) a rhinoceros to run but not jump
   (e) a flounder (living on the sea bottom) to be streamlined
   (f) feathers to have hollow shafts

3. Explain the following:
   (a) Antagonistic muscles are important in the movement of fish.
   (b) Both fish and birds need to be streamlined if they are to move fast.
   (c) The tail fin is not important for forward movement in fish like sea horses and manta rays.
   (d) A bird has an enlarged breastbone called a keel.
   (e) Birds have many hollow bones.
   (f) Animals that move fast often make good food.

4. In your own words explain how
   (a) a bird keeps up
   (b) a bird moves forward in the air
   (c) a fish moves up and down in the water

5. Match the phrases in A with those in B. Write your answers out in full.

| A | B |
|---|---|
| (a) Snakes | allows an animal to move fast as long as it isn't too big. |
| (b) A flexible backbone | are reduced in birds. |
| (c) People | cannot move very fast compared to four-legged animals of the same size. |
| (d) Feathers in birds | have arched feet which help in walking upright. |
| (e) Bones of the hand | or skin in bats make a good wing surface. |

6. Why can't
   (a) a mouse be the size of an elephant?
   (b) an elephant jump?
   (c) swifts fly slowly?
   (d) goldfish swim fast?

7. In some science fiction stories, people go and live in the sea. Sometimes they use lots of equipment, sometimes they change their bodies so they are suited to life in water. Suggest some changes which would make you a better swimmer – in other words, design an aqua-person.

# Exoskeletons- or living in armour

There are many (more than a million) types of animals with soft insides and hard outsides, or **exoskeletons**. Exoskeletons are built of **chitin**, which is layered like plywood. They have three main advantages:
(a)  they are very strong
(b)  they protect soft tissues
(c)  they stop the animal drying out on land

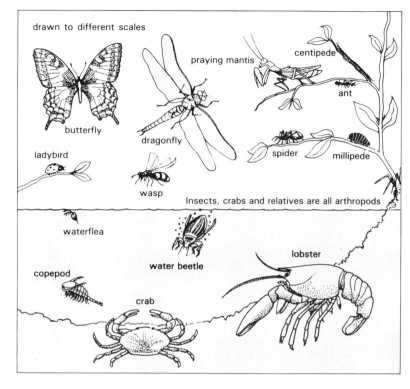

Muscles pull on the exoskeleton in antagonistic pairs – though the layout is a little different from that in vertebrates.

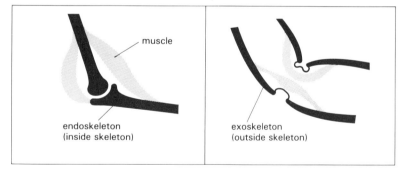

Joints are different in structure but act rather like hinge joints. A crab's claw has several, so it can move in different directions.

Exoskeletons don't stretch. In order to grow, an animal has to shed a layer of chitin and grow while the next layer is hardening. It's a dangerous time and needs a lot of energy. Another problem is that large exoskeletons must be thick and heavy, if they aren't to buckle. Only well-fed crabs and lobsters supported by water get very large.

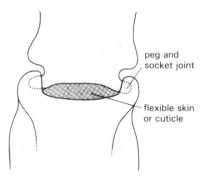

# Green plants and support

Plant cells have walls around them made of cellulose fibres, which don't stretch in mature cells.

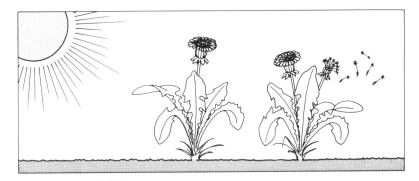

Plants need to hold up leaves, flowers and fruits, so support matters.
They have a system based on the cell.

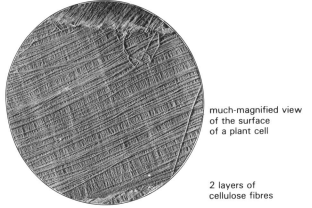

much-magnified view of the surface of a plant cell

2 layers of cellulose fibres

Because it has a cellulose cell wall, a plant cell can be held rigid by pressure from inside, rather like a car tyre. An animal cell would burst. Instead of air, water does the pushing. The pressure per square centimetre is about 2½ times the pressure in a tyre. It's called **turgor** pressure. A cell full of water is said to be **turgid**.

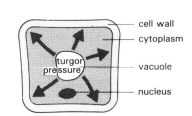

cell wall
cytoplasm
turgor pressure
vacuole
nucleus

Without enough water to keep up the pressure, a plant wilts.

this plant's cells are **not** turgid!

Some cells have extra strengthening materials laid down in various patterns, such as rings or spirals, or in cell corners. Some of the patterns are more complicated.

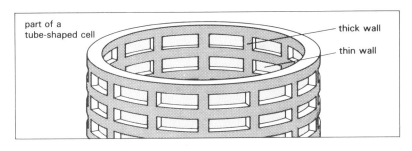

part of a tube-shaped cell

thick wall
thin wall

Strengthened cells often do two jobs – they give support, and they transport materials like water. They are grouped in **vascular bundles** in stems, roots and leaves. It's like the steel in reinforced concrete – great strength for as little weight as possible.

Heavier plants need more support. Vascular bundles join up and develop into wood – which does not rely on full turgor pressure (its cells don't have to be full of water).

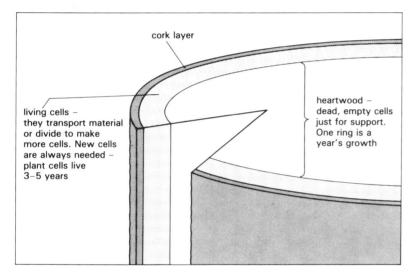

cork layer

living cells –
they transport material
or divide to make
more cells. New cells
are always needed –
plant cells live
3–5 years

heartwood –
dead, empty cells
just for support.
One ring is a
year's growth

vascular bundles –
groups of strengthened cells

cells with
thinner walls

slice of stem

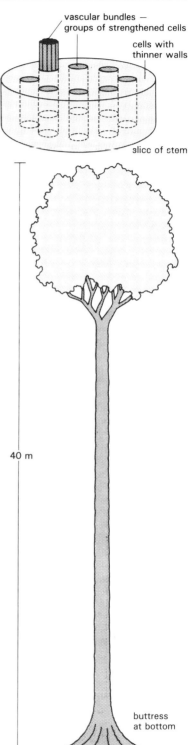

40 m

buttress
at bottom

In tropical rain forests most nutrients are near the surface of the soil. The tree roots, therefore, are also fairly shallow. Really tall trees may need extra support. They have huge buttress roots which may grow four metres out. You may find small buttresses holding up alder trees in a swamp area.

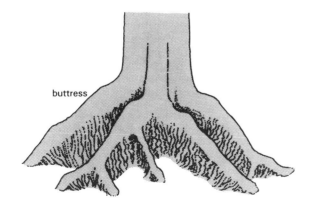

buttress

# Green plants and movement

Most plants, at least as adults, are firmly fixed in place. Only parts of them move. There are two ways that they do it.

## 1. Growth movements

These can be movements away from things or towards them.

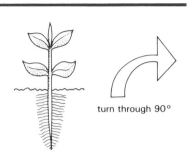

turn through 90°

Shoots grow towards light.

Shoots grow away from gravity, roots towards it.

**Directional** growth (**tropic movement**) involves tips of roots or shoots. Cells in the sides of the tip grow at different rates to cause tropic movements.

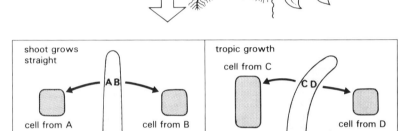

shoot grows straight

cell from A

A B

cell from B

tropic growth

cell from C

C D

cell from D

extra cell growth pushes the shoot in a new direction

## 2. Reversible movements

These are due to temporary changes in cells. Water can be pumped in and out of cells. This is how guard cells open and close pores in leaves.

Movements like this are important in plants where the flowers or leaves open and close during a day. They work the same way in the leaf-collapsing sensitive mimosa.

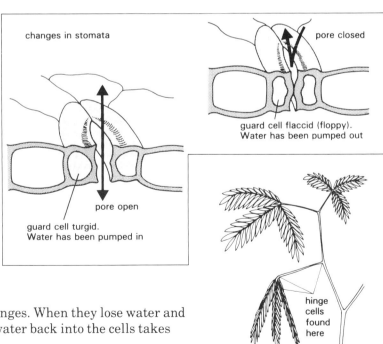

changes in stomata

pore closed

guard cell flaccid (floppy). Water has been pumped out

pore open

guard cell turgid. Water has been pumped in

hinge cells found here

Some cells in the mimosa act as hinges. When they lose water and collapse, the leaf flops. Pumping water back into the cells takes longer (and it needs energy).

# Summary and questions

## Summary

Arthropods have exoskeletons of chitin around their soft tissues. Muscle attachments and joints are different from those of endoskeletons (inside skeletons, of bone or cartilage) but they produce similar movements. Chitin is light and strong in small animals. The amount needed for larger animals rapidly becomes very heavy. Plant support is based on the reinforced cellulose cell wall – this allows water pressure to hold small plants up. Further reinforced cells – wood – hold up larger plants. Plant movements are either tropic (growth) movements, or small reversible changes due to water being moved in and out of cells.

## Questions

1. Fill in the blanks and write the whole thing out.
   Animals with soft insides and hard outsides are said to have _____.
   They include _____ and _____.
   The hard material is called _____, and it is _____ and strong.
   Unfortunately it won't _____ so growth is limited. If an animal becomes too large, this type of skeleton is likely to be too _____.
   This means that large arthropods like _____ and _____ are aquatic, as water helps to support them.

2. (a) What parts of a plant need to be held in the air and why?
   (b) How do the cells on each side of a shoot bending towards light differ?
   (c) Why don't the insides of an arthropod ooze out at the joints?
   (d) Why is the extra supporting material in some cell walls arranged in rings or honeycombs instead of solid sheets?

3. True or false? Write out the following sentences, correcting the ones that are false.
   (a) Plant cells can withstand the same amount of pressure per square centimetre as a car tyre.
   (b) A mimosa leaf collapses when a single 'hinge' cell loses some of its water.
   (d) Dragonflies, waterfleas, spiders, praying mantises, centipedes and butterflies all have exoskeletons.

4. Explain the difference between
   (a) an endoskeleton and an exoskeleton
   (b) antagonistic muscles in an insect's leg and antagonistic muscles in a man's leg
   (c) a peg and socket joint, and a ball and socket joint
   (d) turgid and flaccid

5. Explain what is meant by
   (a) turgor pressure
   (b) vascular bundles
   (c) buttress roots
   (d) tropic movements
   (e) arthropod

6. From the movement point of view, would you rather be an animal with an exoskeleton, or a plant? Why?

7. Reinforced concrete has iron rods inside it which give it strength. It was invented by a gardener called Joseph Monier. It is quite likely that he got the idea from the plants he worked with. Explain how that might be.

8. Why aren't there wasps the size of elephants (as in the monster movies)?

# *Control*

It's no good being able to move if you don't know where you're going, or if you can't react if you do.

The next section is about controlling movement. Cells in general are sensitive to changes around them. Large organisms need the following things:

(a) Special organs sensitive to changes – for example, receivers to tell the difference between light and dark or to pick up noises. Such organs are called **receptors**.

(b) Organs to sort the information and make decisions about what to do. The brain and spinal cord do this in more advanced animals. Insects have bundles of nerves rather than a true brain.

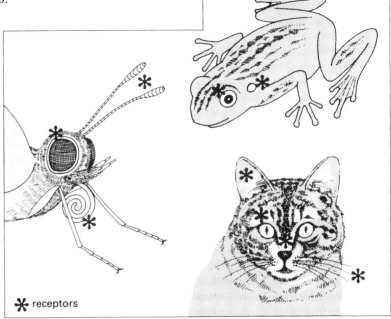

\* receptors

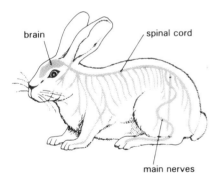

(c) A way of sending messages – whether it's information to the brain or orders to the muscles. The job is done by nerves and chemicals called hormones.

The next few pages are about **receptors.** They look rather different, but they all have
(a) a nerve link to the brain
(b) a good blood supply (even if it's not shown on the diagram)
(c) sensitive cells

Receptors are often in an animal's head (near the brain), pointing in the direction the animal is moving in, and well protected. Animals without brains, such as insects, may have sense organs in unusual places – 'ears' in the legs or wings, for example.

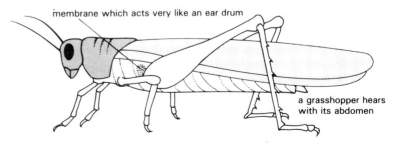

membrane which acts very like an ear drum

a grasshopper hears with its abdomen

Something which triggers a receptor is known as a **stimulus** (plural: stimuli).

| Stimulus | Receptor |
|---|---|
| light | eyes |
| sound | ears |
| pressure | pressure receptors in skin, and lateral line in fish |
| gravity | sacculus and utriculus in ears (more later) |
| head movements | semi-circular canals in ears |
| chemicals in air | nose |
| chemicals in solution | tongue |

bat

potto

pressure receptors in sole of foot

turbot

lateral line

pygmy shrew (3 cm long)

Snakes' tongues carry chemicals in the air to a receptor in the roof of the mouth.

This list doesn't cover everything. We have receptors for heat and cold in our skin. (Rattlesnakes can detect infra-red (warmth) and catch mice in the dark.) Our muscles have stretch receptors to check how far they move. There are nerve endings which signal pain when they are stimulated.

# Skin is a sense organ

Receptors in the skin are nerve endings, wrapped in various ways.

This skin is from the fingers, so no hair is shown. The layer below the epidermis is the **dermis** and below that (just under the pressure receptors) is a layer of fat cells. Blood vessels have been left out.

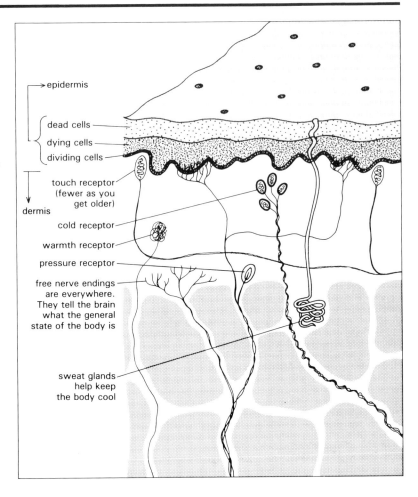

epidermis

dead cells
dying cells
dividing cells

dermis

touch receptor
(fewer as you
get older)

cold receptor

warmth receptor

pressure receptor

free nerve endings
are everywhere.
They tell the brain
what the general
state of the body is

sweat glands
help keep
the body cool

## Choose an ideal injection site

The more receptors in an area of skin, the more sensitive it is. Find the area with the fewest.

Try 1 or 2 points at different distances apart.
Try different bits of skin.
The victim has to guess how many points are touching without looking.

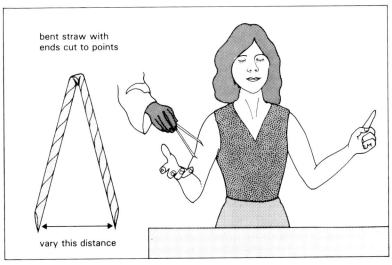

bent straw with
ends cut to points

vary this distance

# The outside of the eye

Light receptors are delicate things – eyes are well protected.

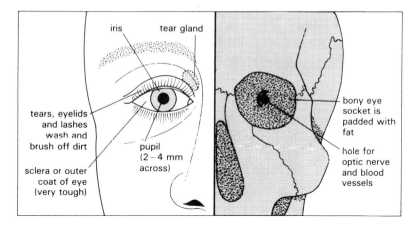

The eye muscles, attached to the eye and eye socket, swing the eyeball around in its socket. They also keep the eye moving very slightly all the time. The brain ignores messages from the eye unless they are always changing. It's like a TV camera rather than a stills camera. Usually it moves so that light from things you are interested in falls on the middle of the light-sensitive cells inside the eye. The **iris** controls the amount of light entering the eye.

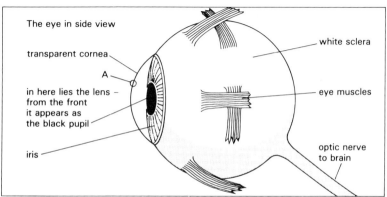

The cornea has its own protective membrane – the conjunctiva.

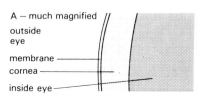

The iris contains muscles which control pupil size.

**Pupil contracted**
Can be as little as 1 mm (-) across

in bright light (helps to protect light-sensitive cells – but sun can still blind you), or with some drugs, e.g. barbiturates and opiates.

**Pupils dilated**
Can be 8 mm (———) across

in dim light, with strong emotions (fear/sex), or with some drugs, e.g. cocaine.

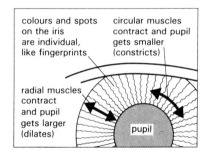

# Inside the eye

The light-sensitive cells are the most important structures inside the eye. There are millions of them in mammalian eyes, arranged in a layer called the **retina**. The cells come in two kinds – rods and cones.

### Rods
You have about 120 million rod cells. They work best in dim light and cannot detect colour. They are mainly found at the edges of the eye. Night animals have extra rods.

### Cones
You have about 7 million cones. They give you colour vision but are not sensitive to dim light. Many are clustered in the middle of the back of your eye. Animals with colourful mates or food are likely to have extra cones.

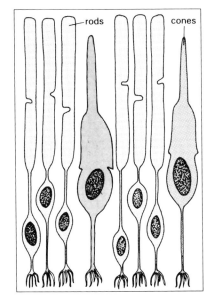

Other parts of the eye are devoted to making sure a sharp image falls on the retina, to protecting it, and to taking messages from the receptor cells to the brain.

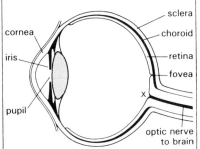

X is the blind spot. It has no sensitive cells – only nerve fibres to the brain. In the centre of the eye is the fovea – the most sensitive part, where most cone cells are.

The **choroid** contains blood vessels which supply the inner eye with food and oxygen. It is dark in colour to absorb light and stop light rays reflecting around inside the eye. The blood vessels leave the eye at the same place as the optic nerve.

The two **humours** fill the eyeball and help keep it in shape. Glaucoma is caused by having too much fluid in the eye. It hurts and can cause blindness if untreated.

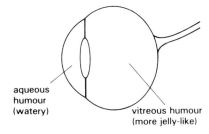

### Judging distances and looking for danger
Some animals have their eyes on the sides of their heads. As a result they see different things with each eye, and they can see a great deal of the area around them. This is useful to animals which are hunted.

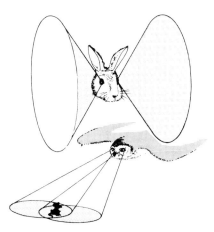

Hunting animals and ones which jump from tree to tree are more likely to have their eyes on the front of the head. This allows them to judge distance. To look at the same object, the eyes have to turn in. The closer the object, the more turning is needed. You'll see this if you look at the tip of your nose. Your brain uses the amount of turning to work out distance. The slightly different views seen by each eye also give a 3-D view of the world.

**Accommodation**, or focusing, is important because light from any point you look at is spreading out. Light rays from the point must be bent if you are to see it clearly.

Most of this is done by the cornea, while fine focusing is done by the lens. Light from a distant object needs less bending to focus it. A thinner lens can do the job.

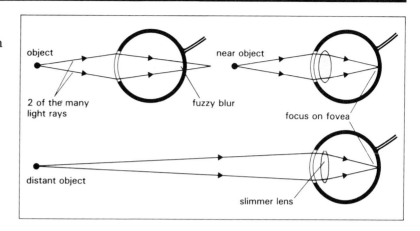

When you are young, your lenses are fairly soft and can change shape easily. The shape of the lens depends upon the muscles which hold it in position. It goes stiff with age and the muscles may also become weaker. Because of this, older people may not be able to focus on near objects easily. They need glasses for reading.

### The ciliary muscles and accommodation
*Near objects*
The muscles of the ciliary body contract and pull on the sclera – not the lens. The sclera gives a little and this lessens the pull on the fibres. The lens becomes rounder and can bend light more.

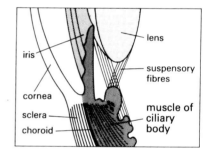

*Far objects*
The ciliary muscles relax. The scleroid pulls at the fibres. The fibres pull the lens thinner. Light is bent less.

Images of objects are upside down on the retina. The coded signals to the brain have to be 'turned over'.

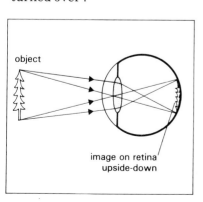

**Problems** may occur if the eyeball is not a perfect sphere.

**Long sight – short eyeball**
Light from near objects falls behind the retina.
A converging lens helps – it starts bending the light before it reaches the eye.

**Short sight – long eyeball**
Light from distant objects focuses in front of the retina.
A diverging lens helps – spreads light further out so that it focuses on the retina.

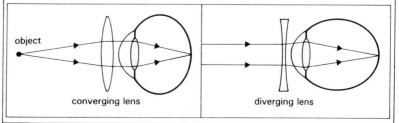

37

# The ear and sound

Ears change vibrations in the air into nerve signals to the brain. It's a change from physical movement to electrical messages the brain can understand. How is it done?

### The outer ear
Some animals have no outer ear – just an exposed ear drum.

ear drum

In any case, the ear drum moves when sound waves hit it.

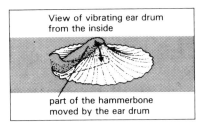

View of vibrating ear drum from the inside

part of the hammerbone moved by the ear drum

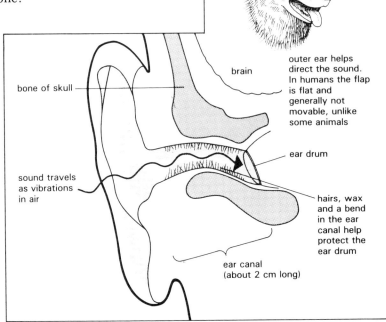

brain

bone of skull

sound travels as vibrations in air

outer ear helps direct the sound. In humans the flap is flat and generally not movable, unlike some animals

ear drum

hairs, wax and a bend in the ear canal help protect the ear drum

ear canal (about 2 cm long)

### The middle ear

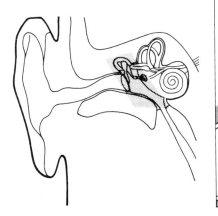

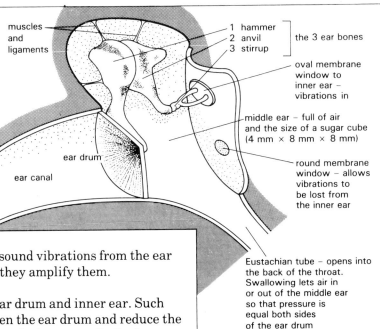

muscles and ligaments

ear drum

ear canal

1 hammer
2 anvil
3 stirrup

the 3 ear bones

oval membrane window to inner ear – vibrations in

middle ear – full of air and the size of a sugar cube (4 mm × 8 mm × 8 mm)

round membrane window – allows vibrations to be lost from the inner ear

Eustachian tube – opens into the back of the throat. Swallowing lets air in or out of the middle ear so that pressure is equal both sides of the ear drum

The ear bones can move and carry sound vibrations from the ear drum to the inner ear. On the way they amplify them.

Very loud noises can damage the ear drum and inner ear. Such noises trigger muscles which tighten the ear drum and reduce the push by the stirrup on the window to the inner ear. In the long run, loud noises will reduce the sensitivity of the ear.

**The inner ear**
This is the tricky bit.

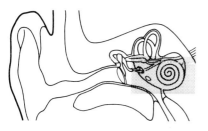

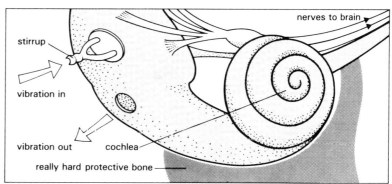

The **cochlea** (which means 'snail') is a membrane bag full of fluid, floating in cushioning fluid. It really is snail-shaped – 5 mm high and 9 mm across at the base. What happens inside?

Inside the cochlea are two layers of membrane joined by sensitive cells.

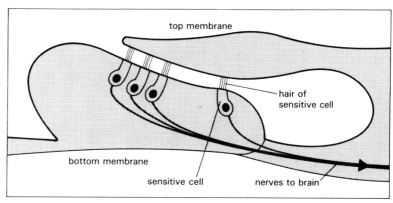

If the membranes bend, they move relative to each other and the hairs are pulled. This triggers the sensitive cells to send a message to the brain.

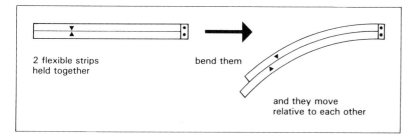

The membranes run around the coil of the 'snail'.

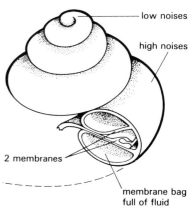

Membranes near the bottom of the cochlea's coil bounce and bend to the fast vibrations of high noises. Those at the top of the coil move to slow vibrations – low noises.

Young humans can hear frequencies of 20 (low) to 20 000 (high) cycles per second. Many animals can hear much higher noises. They use them for everything from calling mother (baby mice) to working out where they are and where food is (bats).

# Gravity

The inner ear isn't just used for hearing. It also helps you to keep your balance. When it is confused you become dizzy.

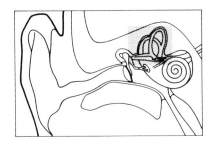

## Which way is down?

The brain answers this question using information from the **utriculus**. Receptors are sensory cells with hairs embedded in a jelly. In the jelly are chalk grains.

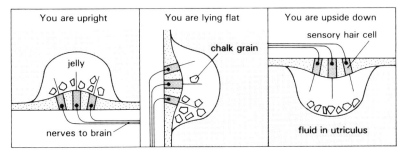

You are upright

jelly

nerves to brain

You are lying flat

chalk grain

You are upside down

sensory hair cell

fluid in utriculus

## Head movements

These need to be taken into account. Receptors at the base of the **semi-circular canals** help here.

The semi-circular canals are three fluid-filled tubes at right angles to each other. The bulge at the base of each canal is an **ampulla**. Whichever way the head moves, fluid will move in at least one of the canals. The three directions can be shown by three fingers held at right angles.

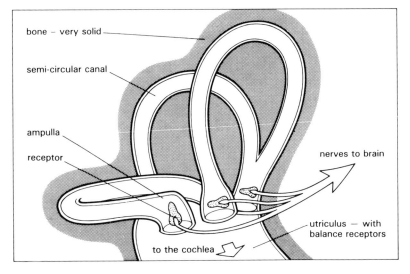

bone – very solid

semi-circular canal

ampulla

receptor

nerves to brain

utriculus — with balance receptors

to the cochlea

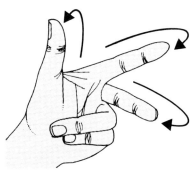

The receptors contain a jelly which is heavier than the fluid in the canals. It drags on the hairs when the fluid moves.

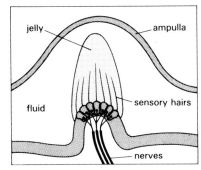

jelly

ampulla

fluid

sensory hairs

nerves

40

# Summary and questions

## Summary

In order to survive, organisms must know something about changes in the world around them. They have receptors – groups of cells sensitive to changes. Stimulus is a word for any change which affects a particular receptor. So far we have heard about:

| the senses of | the receptor | the stimuli |
|---|---|---|
| sight | eye | light |
| hearing | ear | sound |
| balance | ear | gravity and movement |
| touch | skin | pressure |

There are more to come.

## Questions

1. In the text there were no large completely labelled diagrams of the eye or the ear – because they take up a lot of room and are a bit much all at once. However, you now have all the information needed to draw these diagrams, and you should have them in your notes.

   Use a whole page for each diagram of a slice through the eye or the ear.

   On the eye you should label:
   lens, ciliary muscles, retina, blind spot, **pupil, iris, choroid, sclera, retina, fovea,** optic nerve, cornea, eyelid, eyelash, eye muscles, aqueous humour, vitreous humour.

   On the ear you should label:
   inner ear, middle ear, outer ear, earlobe, ear canal, ear drum, hammer, anvil, stirrup, oval window, round window, Eustachian tube, utriculus, semicircular canals, cochlea, nerves to brain, fluid, bone.

   It may help to do a rough sketch first to make sure everything fits in. Use one colour for bones, another for liquids, and so on to reduce confusion.

2. Explain
   (a) why **three** semi-circular canals are needed
   (b) why you think that the inner ear has such hard bones to protect it
   (c) how the ear protects itself from damage by loud noises
   (d) the job of the Eustachian tube

3. Match the part of the eye with the job it does. Write out full sentences.

   | Part of eye | Job |
   |---|---|
   | The sclera | takes information to the brain. |
   | The choroid | protects the eye surface. |
   | The retina | allows light into the eye. |
   | The membrane over the cornea | changes the lens shape for focusing. |
   | The optic nerve | is the outer tough coat. |
   | The cornea | absorbs light and contains blood vessels |
   | The ciliary body | contains cells sensitive to light. |

4. Explain the difference between the following (give examples):
   (a) a receptor and a stimulus
   (b) a dilated pupil and a contracted pupil
   (c) the sense organs in the dermis and epidermis of skin
   (d) the lens shape for focusing near objects and its shape for focusing far ones

5. When you have a bad cold, you sometimes get a dripping nose. The drip includes a lot of liquid from your tear glands – the liquid runs down into the back of your nose. Alexander Fleming grew bacteria on agar jelly as part of his research. He noticed that where these nose drips landed, the bacteria died. What does this suggest about the way tears protect your eyes?

# Chemicals-tasting and smelling

The senses of taste and smell are both involved with chemicals. Chemicals in food are detected mostly in the mouth. Chemicals in the air are picked up by noses – though insects as usual don't follow the rules.

bluebottle

Bluebottles (blow flies) have chemical receptors in the mouth **and** legs.

## Smell

Smells vary a lot. It is not clear exactly how the receptors work, but smell is an important part of taste. Try eating mashed apple and mashed onion while holding your nose. It's not easy to tell the difference. Smell matters in sorting good food from bad, in avoiding poisons, and in sex. Some animals find their mates by smell, and for many smell triggers sexual behaviour. (It's important for humans, too.)

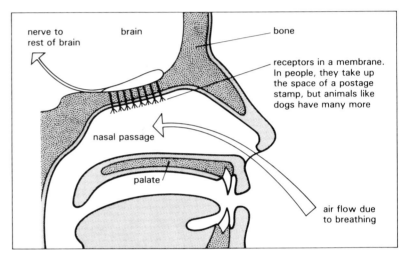

nerve to rest of brain

brain

bone

receptors in a membrane. In people, they take up the space of a postage stamp, but animals like dogs have many more

nasal passage

palate

air flow due to breathing

In close-up, the receptor cells look like this.

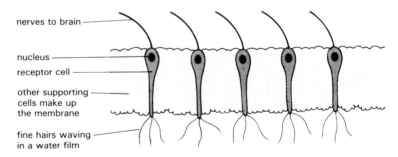

nerves to brain

nucleus

receptor cell

other supporting cells make up the membrane

fine hairs waving in a water film

Inside, the nose is damp. The chemicals in the air dissolve in a film of liquid on top of the receptor cells. Chemicals which dissolve in fat also trigger the receptor cells. Very small amounts of air-borne chemicals can be picked up.

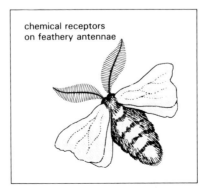

chemical receptors on feathery antennae

Male silkworm moths can find a female 2 km away by scent alone.

## Taste

You taste less than you think. Only four basic kinds of flavour really affect the tongue – sour, bitter, sweet and salty.

Not all the tongue is sensitive to chemicals, and some areas are sensitive to particular tastes.

### Taste map of the tongue

Work out a way of checking your own tongue. This pattern can vary a lot – your tongue may be different.

The receptors are called **taste buds** and are found on the sides of small bumps called **papillae**.

Section through a papilla

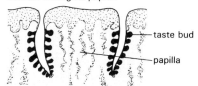

taste bud

papilla

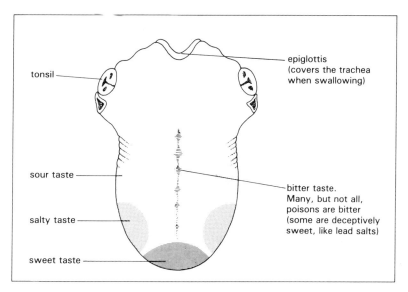

tonsil

epiglottis (covers the trachea when swallowing)

sour taste

salty taste

sweet taste

bitter taste. Many, but not all, poisons are bitter (some are deceptively sweet, like lead salts)

Taste buds are sensitive to chemicals dissolved in water – solid salt has no taste. Taste buds can 'change taste' – perhaps because the cells in them do not live long. New and perhaps different cells are always being added to taste buds as replacements.

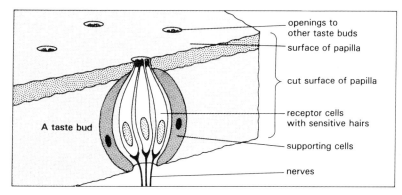

openings to other taste buds

surface of papilla

cut surface of papilla

receptor cells with sensitive hairs

supporting cells

nerves

A taste bud

Taste buds don't have to be inside. The sturgeon has taste buds on the underside of its snout. They are used to sense food on the bottom of the river.

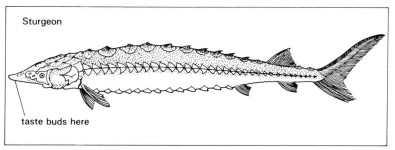

Sturgeon

taste buds here

# Plants and stimuli

Do plants have special sense organs? What kinds of stimuli can they react to?

## Light

A leafy shoot grows towards the light. A young plant grows faster without any light.

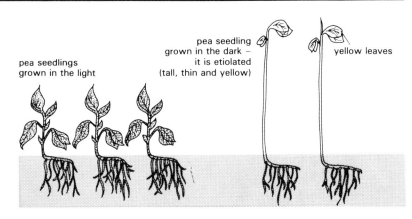

pea seedling grown in the dark – it is etiolated (tall, thin and yellow)

yellow leaves

pea seedlings grown in the light

Cells at the growing tip respond to light. A plant in a light-proof collar will bend, if the tip is in the light. A plant with a light-proof cap won't bend.

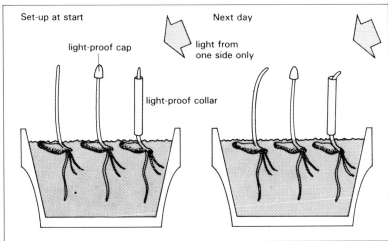

Set-up at start

Next day

light-proof cap

light from one side only

light-proof collar

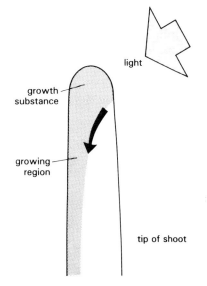

light

growth substance

growing region

tip of shoot

The experiment shows that the cells at the tip are affected by the light, but cells a little further back are the ones that react.

It probably works like this: a growth substance is made at the tip. This travels down the shaded side of the plant to the growing region, where it causes cells to grow and bend the plant.

Growth reactions or tropisms (this one is **phototropism**) can be towards the stimulus or away from it. Growth towards the stimulus is said to be **positive**. Shoots show positive phototropism. Growth away is called **negative**. Roots show negative phototropism.

## Gravity

A buried seed has no light to guide it. **Geotropism** – growth in response to gravity – results in shoots growing up and roots growing down.

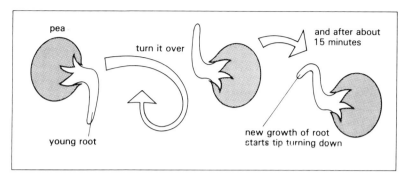

The response is quite fast. It seems that in plant cells there are particles heavy enough to sink to the bottom of the cell, whichever side that is. This shows the cell which way is down. However, cells can be fooled.

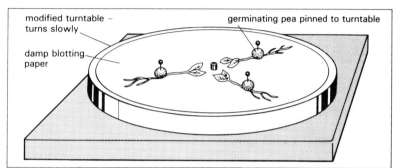

In plants grown on a turntable, shoots grow towards the centre, roots away from it. From the plant's point of view the middle of the turntable is 'up' and the edge is 'down'.

## Not all stimuli produce tropic reactions

Touch causes mimosa leaves to flop. Venus' fly-traps close on flies. The stimulus is touch, again, but one tap is not enough. The sensitive hairs of the leaf need to be stimulated several times in a short time, quite lightly – just like a fly blundering around on the leaf.

The leaves of plants like chrysanthemums react to the pattern of light and darkness (that is, how long the days are). This triggers the plant to flower at the right season. Covering the growing tips makes no difference – it's the leaves that detect the light periods.

Plants may not have special sense organs but they do have many cells sensitive to stimuli.

They may only be able to respond to stimuli very simply. With light, for example, they may only react to its direction, or to the fact it's there. Many animals do this too, if they only have light-sensitive cells instead of proper eyes.

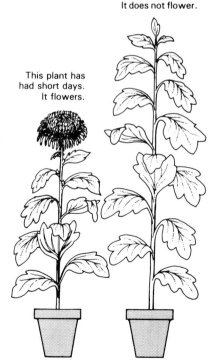

This plant has had long days. It does not flower.

This plant has had short days. It flowers.

45

# Summary and questions

## Summary

Plants and animals can react to change in their environment such as changes in light and sound. Such changes are called stimuli and are detected by receptors which contain sensitive cells. Receptors include eyes, ears, tongues, noses and skin in animals. In plants, cells at growing tips respond to stimuli with tropic reactions. Other cells are also sensitive.

## Questions

1.  Pick an animal other than a human or a pet, and explain how it uses its senses to
    (a) choose a suitable place to live (not too hot or cold, safe from predators and so on)
    (b) find food
    (c) communicate with others of its own kind – for example when choosing a mate

2.  You have fried bacon for breakfast. Copy and fill in this table which describes the event. The first part is done for you.

| Event | Stimulus | Receptor |
|---|---|---|
| seeing the bacon | light | eye |
| feeling the bacon as you take it out of its wrapping | | |
| hearing the bacon cooking | | |
| smelling the bacon | | |
| feeling the hot bacon once it's cooked | | |
| eating the bacon | | |

3.  The sense of smell is better developed in some organisms than it is in people. Dogs are an example. However, smells are important to us – make a list of things at home which have been bought for their smell. For example, most spices are to make food smell better and encourage people to eat it.

4.  It's useful to have more than one sense because the different senses have different advantages and disadvantages. For example – light travels fast and you can see things at a distance. But light doesn't travel round corners. Give one advantage and one disadvantage of each of these senses:
    (a) hearing
    (b) smell
    (c) touch
    (d) taste

5.  Explain the difference between the following pairs (use examples and pictures):
    (a) chemical receptors in the nose and chemical receptors in the tongue
    (b) a papilla and a taste bud
    (c) the appearance of a pea seedling grown in the dark and one grown in the light
    (d) geotropism and phototropism
    (e) a positive tropism and a negative tropism

6.  (a) Explain why shoots grow up even in the dark. Use the following words in your answer: geotropism, phototropism, positive, negative.
    (b) Explain why flowering in plants like chrysanthemum and tobacco is not a tropic reaction. Use the words: sensitive, tip.
    (c) How could you show that plant roots are positively hydrotropic – that is, they grow towards water? Make sure the root is not reacting to light or gravity in your experiment.

# Neurons are nerve cells

Receptors in vertebrates pick up information and pass it on to the brain, which sorts it out and uses it. The information gets to the brain in the same way, whatever the receptor. It travels as tiny **electrical pulses**.

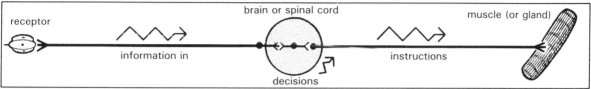

The electrical pulses travel along cells which have become specialized as conductors. They are called **neurons**, and they come in three main shapes.

**Axons** and **dendrons** are the long part of a neuron. They can be very long. For example, there are dendrons which run from a fingertip to the spinal cord. Dendrons carry electrical impulses towards the cell body. Axons carry impulses away from the cell body.

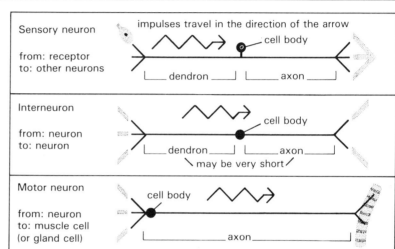

These extensions of cells are very thin and fragile. **Nerves** are bundles of axons and dendrons in a protective coat.

Many animals have axons and dendrons insulated with fat. Electrical impulses move faster along axons and dendrons which are insulated. If an animal loses its insulation, something very like a short circuit happens, and control of the muscles is lost. This sometimes happens as the result of disease.

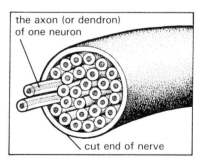

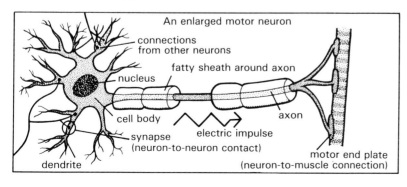

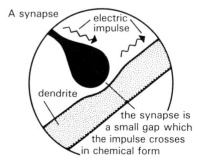

# The central nervous system

Animals with a central nervous system (CNS) have fast complicated reactions to changes around them. The CNS is a tube made up of a network of neurons and other cells. Bulges grow and fold at one end to form a brain. The CNS is connected to the rest of the body by nerves.

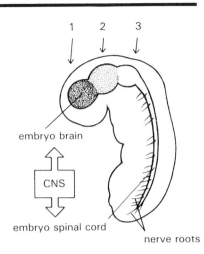

The embryo brain looks much the same in all vertebrates (animals with backbones). It has three bulging areas:
1. forebrain
2. midbrain
3. hindbrain

In animals like the frog each part is roughly equal in the adult. Each of the lobes has its own job, and receives information from particular sense organs.

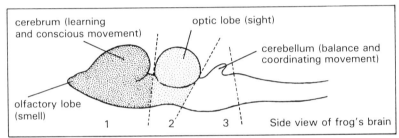

The importance of the different lobes is related to size. In humans the cerebrum is huge. It has folds to provide extra surface for neuron cell bodies. These give the brain its grey colour.

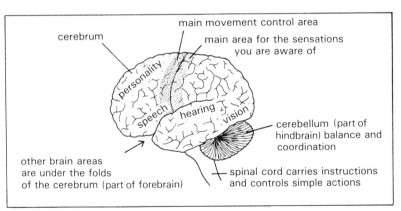

I think, therefore I am.

Mapping the brain is difficult. Patients having brain surgery can help by reporting what it feels like when parts of the brain are electrically stimulated. (It doesn't hurt – the brain has no receptors that signal pain.) Also, patients with brain injuries lose abilities which often relate to which part of the brain is damaged. There are few patients to study and it is hard to be certain exactly what is being studied. The results are sometimes surprising. A few of them are on the next page.

The brain has two halves and the two halves do not always do things equally well.

The left side of the brain controls the right side of the body, and the right the left.

The areas sending conscious instructions to muscles and receiving information consciously are not equally divided among the parts of the body.

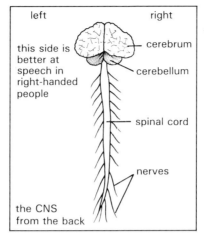

left    right

this side is better at speech in right-handed people

cerebrum

cerebellum

spinal cord

nerves

the CNS from the back

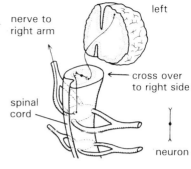

nerve to right arm

left

cross over to right side

spinal cord

neuron

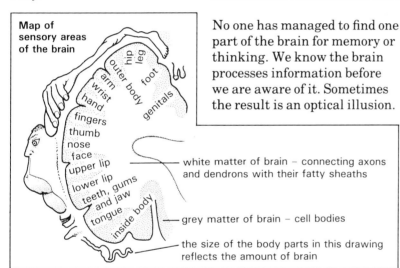

Map of sensory areas of the brain

leg
hip
outer body
foot
arm
wrist
hand
genitals
fingers
thumb
nose
face
upper lip
lower lip
teeth, gums and jaw
tongue
inside body

white matter of brain – connecting axons and dendrons with their fatty sheaths

grey matter of brain – cell bodies

the size of the body parts in this drawing reflects the amount of brain

No one has managed to find one part of the brain for memory or thinking. We know the brain processes information before we are aware of it. Sometimes the result is an optical illusion.

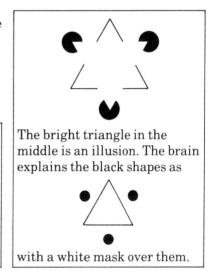

The bright triangle in the middle is an illusion. The brain explains the black shapes as

with a white mask over them.

We can also study the small electrical currents that flow through the brain all the time. Electrodes taped to the skull can pick them up. People vary a lot, but the patterns on the right (an electro-encephalogram or EEG) from a normal brain are fairly typical. EEGs are useful in detecting epilepsy.

The currents are the result of many chemical changes in brain cells. Mental illnesses, like many other illnesses, may partly be caused by some of the chemical reactions getting out of balance.

The mammalian brain is well protected and so complex that many scientists prefer to work with simpler animals. They hope that information from them can be used one day to help explain more complex brains.

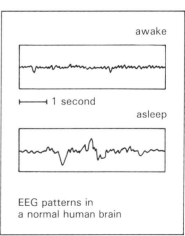

awake

1 second

asleep

EEG patterns in a normal human brain

# Nervous systems in action

Muscles contract when stimulated by nerves. Simple nerve nets with sensory and receptor nerves can control movement.

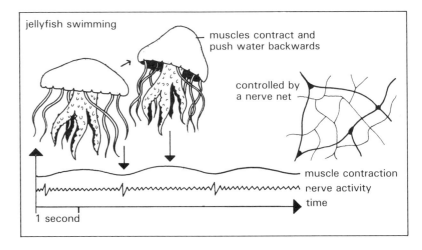

Animals like earthworms with a 'head' end have a more organized nervous system than a jellyfish. The 'brain' of a worm is not needed for complex learning (unlike mammals) but is important in controlling the rate of body reactions.

| Activity | Whole animal | Without 'brain' |
|---|---|---|
| mating | normal | same as normal |
| reaction to light | moves away from bright light | moves towards bright light |
| simple learning, e.g. moving towards food | normal | same as normal |
| overall activity | normal | increases |

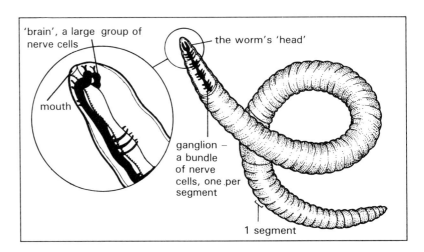

Vertebrates have much more complex systems. The brain is needed to organize the many neurons involved in activities like reading or playing football. Some simple activities may involve fewer neurons.

The simplest reaction in humans is a reflex. It involves at least three neurons. Below is a description of the knee jerk reflex. Most reflexes (like pulling a finger away from a hot stove) are more complicated than this.

1. The tendon below the knee is tapped. This stretches the tendon and the muscles in the thigh. Receptors in the muscles are stimulated and send a signal to the central nervous system (CNS).
2. The impulse crosses the spinal cord as an interneuron is triggered.
3. The interneuron triggers a motor neuron which stimulates a muscle – and the knee jerks.
   (Interneurons also have connections to the brain – so you know the knee is jerking, but you can't stop it.)

sensory neuron

stretch receptor in muscle

section through spinal cord

motor end plate linking muscle and motor neuron

tendons attached to bone at the bottom and muscle at the top

Mammals also have nerves involved in controlling body activities rather than body movement. Neurons of the **autonomic nervous system** go to heart, lungs, liver, glands and gut. One set of nerves speeds up useful body processes like the heartbeat when there is an emergency – danger about. Another set slows things down, returning the body to normal when the danger is past. These nerves come from the hind brain and spinal cord.

Most people cannot control their autonomic nervous system – but there are exceptions.

Many drugs affect the autonomic nervous system. Nicotine (in cigarettes), caffeine (in coffee, tea and cola) and amphetemines are stimulants – like danger. Alcohol, barbiturates, tranquilizers and opiates (heroin & co.) push the system in the opposite direction. They are depressants, and addictive into the bargain.

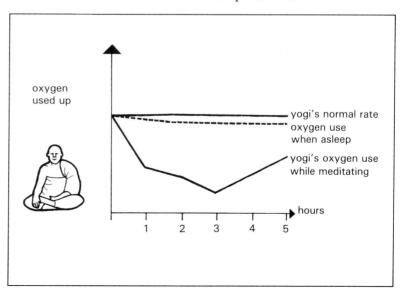

oxygen used up

yogi's normal rate oxygen use when asleep

yogi's oxygen use while meditating

hours

1  2  3  4  5

# Animal hormones

Some body activities are not easy to control with nervous impulses. Growth, for example, takes a lot of time and involves many cells in a complicated pattern of changes. Chemical messages between cells keep the body acting as a whole. The chemicals which form the messages are called **hormones**. They are mainly made by groups of cells called **ductless** or **endocrine glands**. Hormones are carried away from ductless glands and around the body in the blood. Each hormone affects particular tissues and organs in its own way.

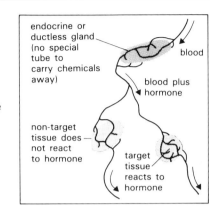

Here are four examples of hormones. Note how important it is to have the right amount of a hormone.

## 1. Thyroxin

This is made in the thyroid gland. In humans it controls the rate of energy production and reactions in cells generally. Too much thyroxin and you are over-active; too little and you are sluggish. In animals such as frogs, thyroxin controls the changes of metamorphosis.

Iodine is an important part of a thyroxin molecule.

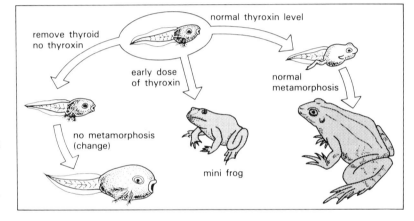

## 2. Insulin

This is made in the pancreas. It allows the body to use sugar efficiently. It increases glucose storage in the liver and allows other cells to take in glucose. It is especially important after a meal when the glucose level in the blood rises. Too little insulin and glucose reaches high levels in the blood. The kidney gets rid of insulin and the body can run out of glucose. This is one form of diabetes.

## 3. Adrenalin

This is made in the adrenal glands. Along with part of the autonomic nervous system, adrenalin prepares the body for action.

Adrenalin promotes:
wider air passages (lets more air in)
extra glucose in the blood (for energy)
faster heartbeat
more blood to brain and muscles
the dilation of pupils (lets more light into the eye)
less blood to gut
hair standing on end (makes an animal look bigger)

## 4. Sex hormones

These are made by the ovary (oestrogens) or testes (androgens). They are involved in the growth of secondary sexual characteristics, such as wider hips and larger breasts (women) or beards, broader shoulders and deeper voices (men). Taking these hormones away can have a dramatic effect.

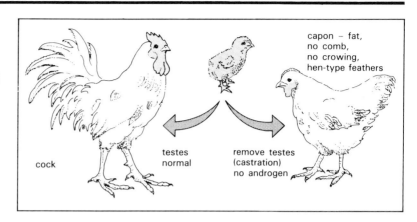

cock

testes normal

remove testes (castration) no androgen

capon – fat, no comb, no crowing, hen-type feathers

The leader of the endocrine glands is the **pituitary**. It makes hormones which control the other ductless glands, and is affected by chemical messages from other parts of the body.

The pituitary is a bulge in the base of the brain. It is connected to the brain by both blood vessels and nerves. It provides a link between hormone control and nervous control.

The two systems have different strengths and weaknesses. Between them they control movement, energy supply, waste removal, growth and repair of the body.

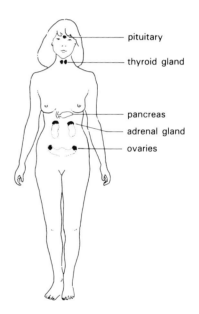

- pituitary
- thyroid gland
- pancreas
- adrenal gland
- ovaries

human brain (sliced to show the pituitary, which would otherwise be hidden by the bulging cerebrum)

### The two systems

|  | The endocrine system | The nervous system |
|---|---|---|
| consists of | ductless glands | a network of neurons |
| The messages are | chemicals – hormones | electrical pulses |
| They are transported | in blood | along axons and dendrons |
| Speed of action is | slow (minutes) except adrenalin | fast (less than a second) |
| Effects are triggered by | changes inside and outside the body | |
| and last | quite a long time | a short time |
| Typical jobs (though these overlap) are | growing, regulating salt and sugar concentrations in the body | walking, flying, picking things up, controlling breathing rate |

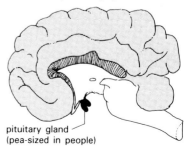

pituitary gland (pea-sized in people)

# Plant hormones

Plants too have hormones – chemicals which control activities. The first to be discovered were the **auxins**, which are important in tropic movements.

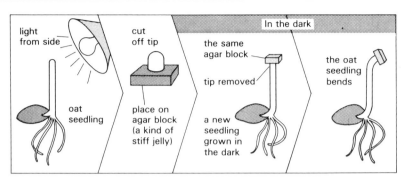

This works with auxins from many types of plants. There must be a chemical controlling the growth. It can't be a nerve, they don't work if they are cut. The dark side of the seedling produces lots of auxin, the light side not so much. The auxin diffuses into the agar and then into the new plant. Where there is a lot of auxin, the cells grow faster.

Auxins affect different parts of the plant differently.

Like animal hormones, plant hormones may travel quite large distances in a plant.

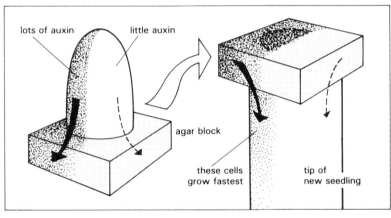

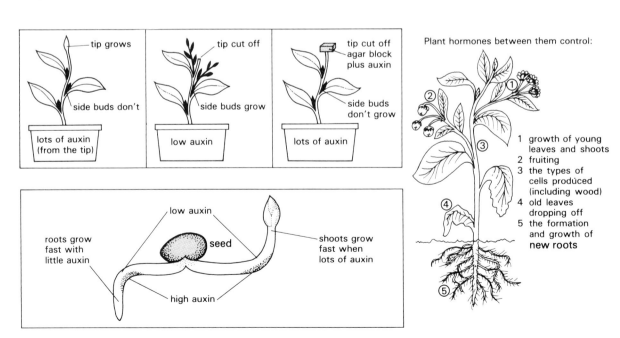

Plant hormones between them control:

1 growth of young leaves and shoots
2 fruiting
3 the types of cells produced (including wood)
4 old leaves dropping off
5 the formation and growth of **new roots**

# Summary and questions

## Summary
The workings of an animal's body are coordinated by means of nerves and hormones. There are three main types of nerve cells (neurons): sensory neurons, interneurons and motor neurons. A reflex action involves three neurons, but more complex actions involve many cells and the control of a brain. The brain plus the spinal cord make up the central nervous system. Hormones are chemicals made by endocrine glands. They pass straight into the blood, which carries them to the tissues they affect. The pituitary is a gland in the brain which helps to co-ordinate nervous and hormonal control.

Chemical communication is important in plants. Many of their growth processes are under hormonal control.

## Questions

1. Make up an advertisement to sell one of the ductless glands to an organism without an endocrine system.

2. Explain in your own words
   (a) endocrine glands
   (b) hormones
   (c) auxins
   (d) castration
   (e) diabetes

3. What does 'I think, therefore I am' mean?

4. Which do you think is more important – the endocrine or the nervous system – when
   (a) a cat catches a mouse
   (b) a kitten grows into a cat

5. Write out the passage below and fill in the blanks.
   A nerve cell or _____ consists of a _____ _____ and a long extension called the _____. Around the extension is a sheath made of _____ which is to _____ it. This is needed because nerve impulses are _____. There are three types of nerve cells called _____ _____, _____ _____ and _____. Connections between nerve cells are called _____ and they involve a gap which the impulse must jump _____. In mammals, the central nervous system or _____ _____ _____ consists of a _____ and a _____ _____. Not all animals have a central nervous system – for example a _____ does not.

6. Match the structures in A with the jobs they do in B. Write out full sentences.

   | A | B |
   | --- | --- |
   | The cerebrum | protects the brain. |
   | The cerebellum | is important in learning, thought and controlled movements. |
   | The spinal cord | is important in balance and co-ordination. |
   | The skull | carrys instructions and is important in reflex actions. |

7. (a) The constriction of the pupil when a bright light is shone into the eye is an example of a reflex. Explain how it might happen.
   (b) Explain why it is so difficult to study how the human brain works.
   (c) Explain why so much of the sensory area of the brain is for the hands and so little for the arms.

8. Answer the following questions, giving a reason in each case:
   (a) Can people choose to control their heart rate – normally under the controls of the autonomic nervous systems?
   (b) Do organisms have to have brains?
   (c) Can a brain with a smooth cerebrum do as many things as a brain with a folded cerebrum?

# Behaviour

All the things a whole organism does make up its behaviour.
Behaviour is aimed at:

obtaining food                 avoiding damage                 breeding.

An organism's activities at any moment depend on many things.

### Instinct and learning

Instinctive behaviour is programmed – inherited with other instructions for building and running the body.

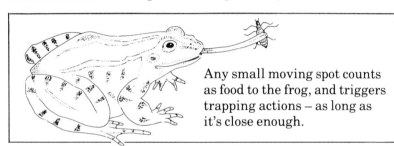

Any small moving spot counts as food to the frog, and triggers trapping actions – as long as it's close enough.

Learning involves changing behaviour. It can be hard to sort it out from instinctive behaviour.

The digger wasp chooses its prey by **instinct** – anything with the right size, shape and smell is food.

Its nest is a hole. It **learns** where the nest is by learning the pattern of rocks and plants around it.

The same applies in higher animals.

A deaf bird will sing some kind of song. To sing is instinctive.

Young birds can learn tunes from birds around them – within limits. Song **pattern** is learned.

## Communicating

Signals between animals are important. Here are some of the things they are used for:

### Finding mates

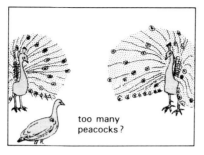

too many peacocks?

### Teaching young

lioness and cub on first hunt

### Avoiding fights

top wolf letting others know

Grrrrr

not-so-top wolf avoiding fight

### Recognizing friends

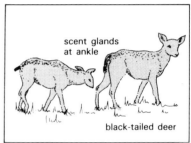

scent glands at ankle

black-tailed deer

Signals can involve scent, sound or sight. They are especially important for **social behaviour**. A group of animals can do more than one animal can. Social behaviour is how they co-operate. Signals help to co-ordinate the group, whether for defence or attack.

musk ox group defence

wolves attack – only effective against single animals

Examples of behaviour go on for ever. Look around and in the rest of this book for more.

**Warning.** Behaviour in the laboratory is often different from an animal's normal behaviour – rather like the effect of exams on your behaviour. It is often best to study behaviour in the wild. However, this can be difficult to do – many organisms are small, fast, rare, hard to find and so on.

# Transport

A passenger list of materials that must move round an organism includes:

- food
- oxygen
- wastes
- hormones

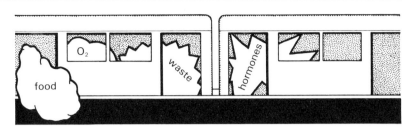

Small organisms don't have much of a problem – nowhere is far from the outside world.

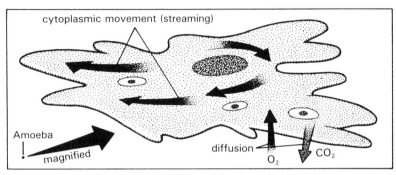

This is not true in larger organisms. Guts and lungs are surfaces where materials can get in and out of an organism by diffusion. They are folded to get a large area into a small space. Most cells are still a long way from those surfaces.

The answer is a blood transport system.

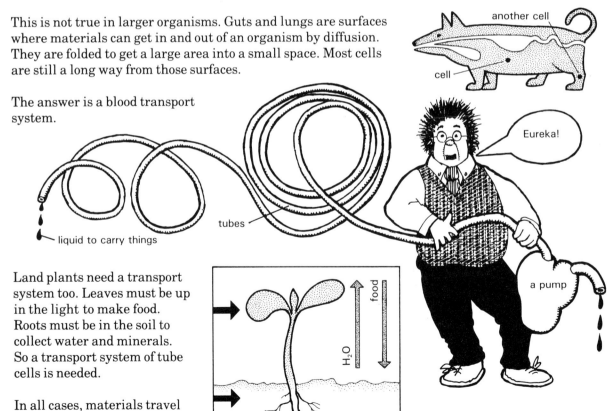

Land plants need a transport system too. Leaves must be up in the light to make food. Roots must be in the soil to collect water and minerals. So a transport system of tube cells is needed.

In all cases, materials travel dissolved in water.

**Diffusion and osmosis** are important in moving water. Both happen in non-living and living systems in the right conditions. They are physical processes.

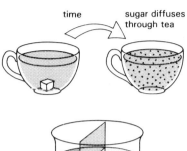

time    sugar diffuses through tea

**Diffusion** you've met before. Particles move at random and end up spread out evenly. A membrane barrier makes no difference as long as it has holes in it big enough for the particles to go through.

**Osmosis** happens when a barrier is **semi-permeable** – that is, it lets some (small) things through but not others (larger particles). It's like a sieve.

Imagine a beaker divided into two by a semi-permeable membrane. Sugar solution is put in one side, water in the other. The holes are big enough for H$_2$O molecules, not for sugar molecules.

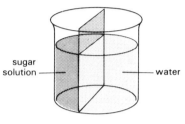

sugar solution    water

This diagram shows the holes, and the water and sugar particles. To begin with there are more water particles on one side than the other.

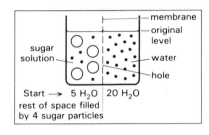

### Time passes
Particles move randomly. Some of the water molecules go through the membrane in both directions.

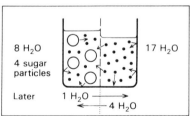

### More time passes
Eventually there are about the same number of water molecules on each side of the membrane. The sugar molecules have to stay on the left.

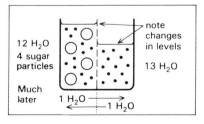

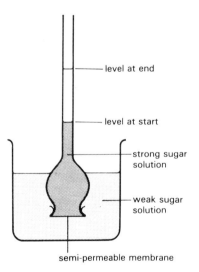

level at end

level at start

strong sugar solution

weak sugar solution

semi-permeable membrane

Osmosis acts against forces like gravity.

The overall effect? Osmosis is the movement of water through a semi-permeable membrane from a dilute solution (or water) to a more concentrated (stronger) one. (It doesn't have to be a sugar solution.)

As you'll see, it is **very** important to living organisms, their transport systems and their cells.

59

# Transport in plants-water and minerals

## The pathway

Small quantities of minerals are taken up by the roots and remain in the plant. They are carried in water which is taken up in enormous amounts. Much of the water absorbed is lost.

The water in soil, plant and air is connected.

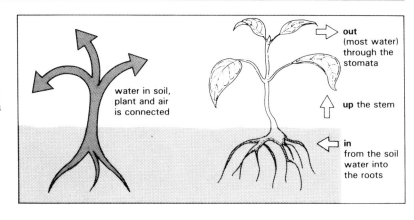

water in soil, plant and air is connected

**out** (most water) through the stomata

**up** the stem

**in** from the soil water into the roots

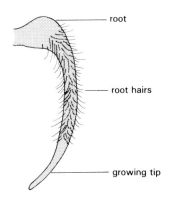

root

root hairs

growing tip

### In

Water comes in through **root hairs**. They provide a large surface area, though they are tiny, because a single plant can have millions of them.

Each root hair is a single cell. The cell sap in them is more concentrated than the soil solution. Water enters a root hair by osmosis (and so makes it more dilute).

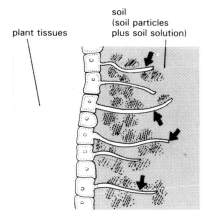

plant tissues

soil (soil particles plus soil solution)

As a result, the root hair cell's sap is now more dilute than the next cell inwards. Water moves into this next cell by osmosis and so on until the transport tubes are reached. Osmosis provides some of the push needed to move the water upwards, but not much.

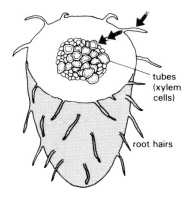

tubes (xylem cells)

root hairs

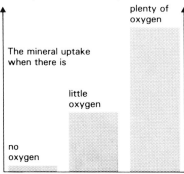

Some evidence for the importance of respiration in mineral uptake

The mineral uptake when there is

plenty of oxygen

little oxygen

no oxygen

Unlike water, minerals don't make their own way into the root hairs. Plants have to pump them in – and use up energy in the process. The energy comes from respiration.

### Up

Water and minerals travel up the stem in **xylem** vessels – hollow tubes. Xylem cells die when they are mature.

To see the xylem vessels, keep a plant in water coloured with vegetable dye. After a while, cut through the stem. The xylem vessels are the groups of dyed cells.

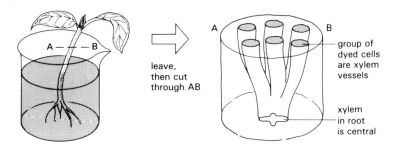

Xylem tubes run up the middle of the root but spread out to form small bundles in the stem. This way they provide more support for the plant, which is their other job. Xylem vessels are very narrow and to some extent water moves up them by **capillarity**.

Water is attracted to the walls of a vessel. In a very narrow (capillary) vessel, the attraction is stronger than the weight of the water. The water moves up the tube. This is capillarity.

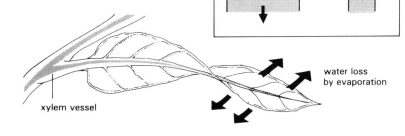

### And out

Water evaporates through pores (stomata) in the leaf. The result is low pressure at the top of the plant, which pulls up more water. This is the most important force which moves water in the xylem vessels. Roots are not essential for water movement.

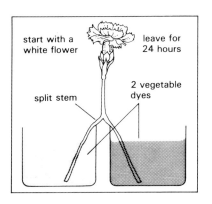

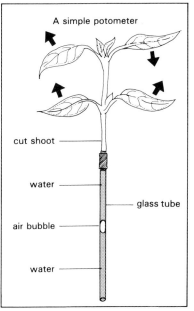

A simple potometer

The rate of water loss (**transpiration**) varies with many things. It can be measured with a potometer. As the plant takes in water, the bubble moves up the glass tube. Its speed depends on the rate of transpiration from the plant's leaves.

Transpiration increases in wind,
bright light,
dry conditions.

Transpiration drops in still air,
the dark,
humid (damp) conditions.

# Transport in plants-food materials

Leaves make sugars. They are transported to flowers, fruit, growing leaves (which need more energy than they can trap) and roots.

Are the same tubes used to transport food materials as water? The answer is NO.

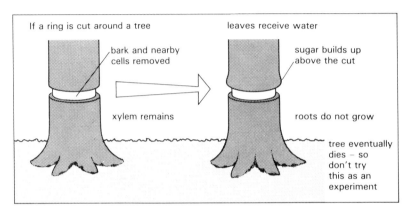

If a ring is cut around a tree

- bark and nearby cells removed
- xylem remains

leaves receive water

- sugar builds up above the cut
- roots do not grow
- tree eventually dies – so don't try this as an experiment

Ringing removes **phloem** cells. These are living tube cells, and together with xylem they form the **vascular tissue** of a plant.

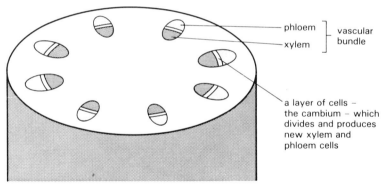

phloem — vascular
xylem — bundle

a layer of cells – the cambium – which divides and produces new xylem and phloem cells

It is difficult to find out what happens in phloem. One method involves aphids.

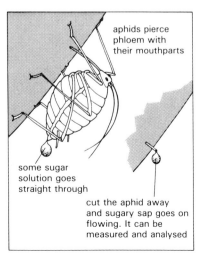

aphids pierce phloem with their mouthparts

some sugar solution goes straight through

cut the aphid away and sugary sap goes on flowing. It can be measured and analysed

Sap from phloem cells contains a lot of sugar, and also amino acids (the sub-units of proteins). Sap in phloem moves up to 100 cm an hour. This is about half the average speed of water in xylem. Unlike xylem cells, phloem cells must be alive for sap movement. Cytoplasmic streaming may help to move food, but it would not be fast enough by itself. Exactly how materials move in phloem is not yet understood.

# Summary and questions

## Summary

Organisms of any size must transport food, oxygen, wastes and hormones around their bodies. This involves a transport system. In plants, this consists of tube cells: xylem and phloem. Water and minerals travel from the roots in xylem cells. Food materials, produced by photosynthesis, are moved in phloem cells from the leaves to the rest of the plant. Phloem cells are living. How materials move in them is not fully understood. Xylem cells are non-living. Liquids are mainly pulled through them by transpiration – the evaporation of water from the leaves. Water enters through root hairs by osmosis. Osmosis is the movement of water through a semi-permeable membrane from a weak solution to a more concentrated one.

## Questions

1. Copy this out, filling in the blanks.
   In plants, water enters through _____ _____ by the process of _____. It travels up the stem to the _____ in tubes called _____. It carries with it _____ _____ which also enter through the roots. The water is pulled up by _____ or the _____ of water from leaf surfaces. Food materials such as _____ and amino acids travel in living cells, the _____ which with the _____ form _____ bundles. It is not really understood what moves the nutrient solution, but it does go to such places as _____, _____ and _____.

2. Explain
   (a) why a cell in the muscle of a dog's leg must be near a transport system
   (b) how you could show that water travels in xylem
   (c) the three ways water is moved in xylem (say which is the most important)
   (d) why ringing eventually kills a tree

3. Explain the difference between
   (a) osmosis and diffusion
   (b) xylem and phloem
   (c) roots and root hairs
   (d) transpiration and ordinary evaporation
   (e) the way water gets into a plant and the way minerals get in

4. What is a potometer?
   Suggest three conditions in which transpiration could be increased.
   Suggest three conditions in which transpiration could be reduced.
   How could you show that any two of your suggestions were correct?

5. (a) The diagrams show a phloem cell and a xylem cell. From what you have read about their functions – the jobs they do – say which you think is which and give a reason for your answer.
   (b) An animal like a cicada which takes food from xylem vessels grows more slowly than an animal like an aphid which feeds from phloem vessels. Why?

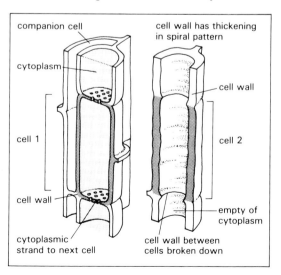

companion cell

cytoplasm

cell 1

cell wall

cytoplasmic strand to next cell

cell wall has thickening in spiral pattern

cell wall

cell 2

empty of cytoplasm

cell wall between cells broken down

# Transport in animals-the blood system

The body fluids in animals transport many things to and from cells – oxygen, food, hormones, heat and wastes. In animals large enough to need one, the blood system contains about a third of the body fluids.

The blood system consists of
**blood**
+
**a pump – the heart**
+
**vessels**

**arteries** – carry blood from the heart
**veins** – carry blood to the heart
**capillaries** – connect arteries and veins

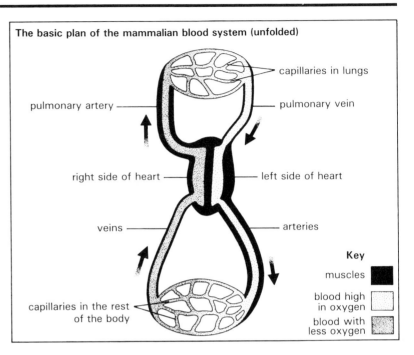

The basic plan of the mammalian blood system (unfolded)

capillaries in lungs

pulmonary artery

pulmonary vein

right side of heart

left side of heart

veins

arteries

capillaries in the rest of the body

**Key**
muscles
blood high in oxygen
blood with less oxygen

## The vessels

**The arteries** are important in distributing blood. During exercise, the arteries to the legs widen and those to the gut constrict (get narrower). This is possible because they have many muscle cells in their walls. These can relax to allow blood through and by peristaltic pumping (like gut muscles) help keep blood moving.

single layer of cells (like a capillary)

layers of muscle and elastic fibres

If the artery walls stiffen, the heart has to work harder. It's the same if the arteries get narrower. This may happen if fatty materials build up on the inner walls of blood vessels. Cholesterol is just one of these fatty materials.

**Arterioles** are the smallest branches of arteries. They control the flow of blood into capillaries, thanks to the smooth muscle cells in their walls. These muscles are controlled by neurons of the autonomic nervous system.

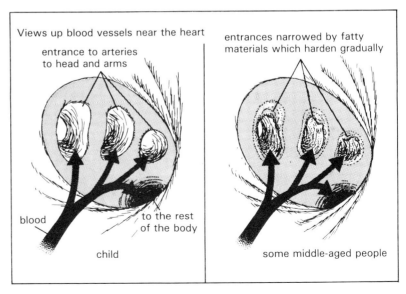

Views up blood vessels near the heart

entrance to arteries to head and arms

entrances narrowed by fatty materials which harden gradually

blood

to the rest of the body

child

some middle-aged people

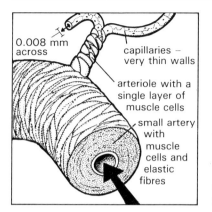

0.008 mm across

capillaries – very thin walls

arteriole with a single layer of muscle cells

small artery with muscle cells and elastic fibres

**Capillaries** are the smallest blood vessels. They wind between body cells. If an artery is a motorway, a capillary is a bicycle path. Their walls are one cell thick, and they leak water and dissolved materials. There are many more capillaries than can be filled at any one time. Only those in areas where blood is most needed contain blood.

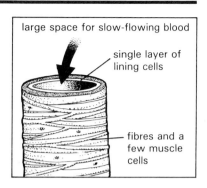

large space for slow-flowing blood

single layer of lining cells

fibres and a few muscle cells

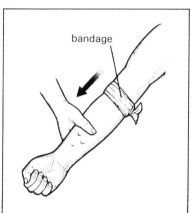

bandage

**Veins** have thinner walls. Veins don't need thick walls because the blood pressure in them is low. They also need to be 'squeezable'. Veins often run through muscles which move bones. As these muscles contract during body movement, they squeeze the veins and push the blood back to the heart. There are valves inside the vein which stop blood flowing the wrong way. The valves are like pockets.

To see the valves:
Tie a tight bandage around someone's arm. (Don't leave it on long.) Stroke blood back towards the hand to make the valves bulge. (Warning: never do this on your own. Bandages can get stuck.)

## Varicose veins

Normally blood returns from the feet to the main veins leading to the heart in veins running up the middle of the leg muscles. Small leg movements are enough to keep the blood moving. There are some small veins near the surface of the leg and usually blood runs from them to the main veins. Valves help.

If you stand still for long periods of time, a problem may build up. Without muscle movements to keep it moving, blood tends to flow back into the surface veins and stretch them. The valves don't shut properly, which makes things worse. Varicose veins are these overstretched and painful surface veins.

Watch out for varicose veins in later life if you are female (about a fifty-fifty chance) or end up in a job with a lot of standing (teaching, hairdressing and so on).

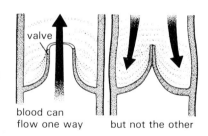

valve

blood can flow one way

but not the other

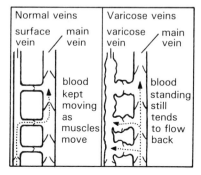

| Normal veins | Varicose veins |
|---|---|
| surface vein / main vein | varicose vein / main vein |
| blood kept moving as muscles move | blood standing still tends to flow back |

# The heart

The heart is a pump – and a very good one at that.

The simplest pump is a length of blood vessel with extra muscle.

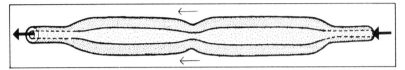

Design Specification – pump for human body

**Must**

work without maintenance for 70 years or more

be self-lubricating

be self-regulating

normal rate 50–70, b. per m.

must cope up to 200 beats per minute

normal volume pumped 5 litres per minute, must cope up to 40 litres per minute

Two such 'hearts' are found in a three-week-old human embryo. To pump more blood, parts of the tube become enlarged. As blood pressure rises, walls become thicker. Valves are needed to stop blood going backwards.

## A single pump – the fish heart

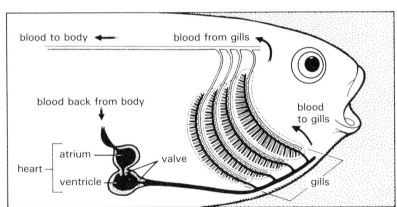

blood to body ← ... blood from gills

blood back from body

heart — atrium / valve

ventricle

blood to gills

gills

One pump is not very efficient. Blood pressure drops in the gills and blood moves slowly round the body. This is fine for a fishy way of life.

## A double pump – the mammalian heart

In mammals there are two pumps. One sends blood to the lungs, the other sends blood to the rest of the body. The right pump and its tubes twist around the left pump and its tubes.

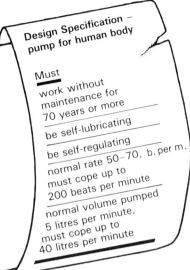

from body    from lungs

R    L

the circles represent one-way valves

A great deal of blood passes through the heart, but its muscles are so thick that they need their own blood supply. Blood for the heart muscles travels through the coronary arteries. Blockage of one of these causes a heart attack.

This means that an area of muscle cells run out of fuel and oxygen, stop contracting and die. This kind of heart problem is called a coronary thrombosis. A thrombosis is a clot. (More later.)

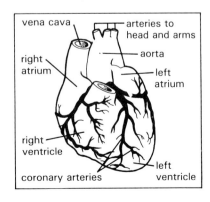

vena cava — arteries to head and arms

right atrium — aorta

left atrium

right ventricle

coronary arteries — left ventricle

## The heartbeat
## First stage

The diagram shows the relaxation phase in the heartbeat. The chambers of the heart fill with blood, which flows from

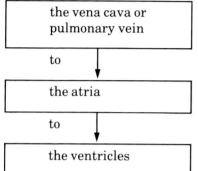

| the vena cava or pulmonary vein |
|---|

to

| the atria |
|---|

to

| the ventricles |
|---|

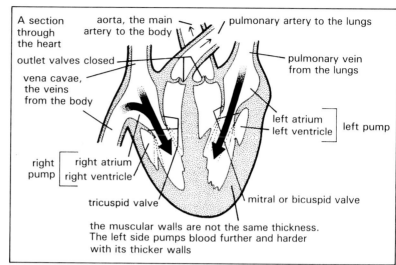

A section through the heart

aorta, the main artery to the body

pulmonary artery to the lungs

outlet valves closed

vena cavae, the veins from the body

pulmonary vein from the lungs

left atrium
left ventricle — left pump

right pump | right atrium
right ventricle

tricuspid valve

mitral or bicuspid valve

the muscular walls are not the same thickness. The left side pumps blood further and harder with its thicker walls

To prevent blood flowing back into the ventricle from the arteries, the aortic and pulmonary valves shut. As they slap shut they make a 'lub' sound. Heart murmurs occur when valves do not shut properly and blood seeps through.

## Second stage
The atria contract

## Third stage
The ventricles contract and push blood up the aorta and pulmonary arteries. The 'dub' sound of the heartbeat is the tricuspid and bicuspid valves slapping shut to prevent blood flowing back into the atria.

The two sets of pumps beat together. The rate at which the heart beats is under the control of the nervous system and adrenalin. It changes as the result of exercise, anger, excitement and so on. The basic rate depends upon the pacemaker, a bundle of cells in the right atrium. It starts a cycle of nervous activity which causes the atria to contract ((a) in the diagram), the ventricles to contract (b), and finally the pacemaker to fire again (c).

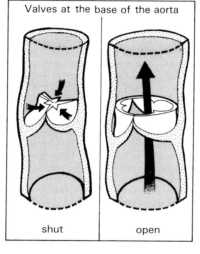

Valves at the base of the aorta

shut          open

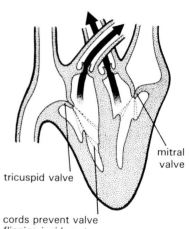

tricuspid valve

mitral valve

cords prevent valve flipping inside out

Contraction phase, stage 3

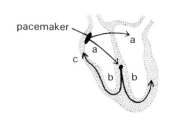

pacemaker
a
c     a
b   b

67

# What is blood?

Blood is made up of plasma, red blood cells, white blood cells and platelets. Plasma is a straw-coloured liquid, mostly water, which does many jobs. Red blood cells transport gases. White blood cells and platelets defend the body.

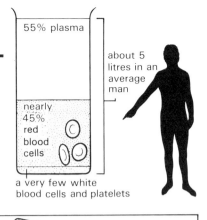

55% plasma

about 5 litres in an average man

nearly 45% red blood cells

a very few white blood cells and platelets

Blood is not isolated in its blood vessels. Some plasma leaks out – and is then called tissue fluid. There is about twice as much tissue fluid in the body as there is blood.

Leaking plasma carries small molecules, such as oxygen and glucose, in solution to body cells. Most of the tissue fluid seeps back into the capillaries, together with dissolved wastes like carbon dioxide.

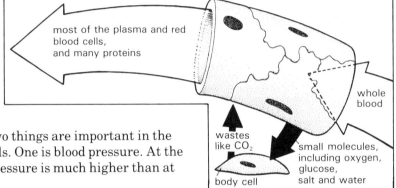

most of the plasma and red blood cells, and many proteins

whole blood

wastes like $CO_2$

body cell

small molecules, including oxygen, glucose, salt and water

How does this return happen? Two things are important in the capillaries which loop around cells. One is blood pressure. At the beginning of such a loop, blood pressure is much higher than at the end of the loop.

The other important thing is osmosis. Because of the proteins in the blood, water tends to move into the capillary by osmosis. When plasma leaves the capillary, large molecules tend to be left behind and so become more concentrated in the blood.

At the start of the capillary loop, blood pressure is more important than osmosis, so the tube leaks. At the end of the loop, blood pressure is much less important than osmosis, so water and small molecules move back into the blood.

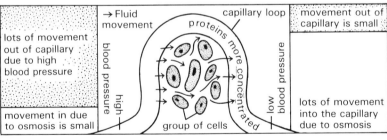

→ Fluid movement

lots of movement out of capillary due to high blood pressure

movement in due to osmosis is small

blood pressure high

proteins more concentrated

capillary loop

group of cells

blood pressure low

movement out of capillary is small

lots of movement into the capillary due to osmosis

Not all the extra tissue fluid goes back into the capillaries. Some is picked up by tiny lymph vessels. The liquid is now called lymph. It moves slowly through the lymph system, and collects white blood cells which help combat infection. Eventually lymph rejoins the blood in the vein at the base of the neck. Blocking

the lymph system causes swelling.

The answer to 'What is blood?' is not simple. Blood is a body fluid that happens to flow in blood vessels, but it is connected to other body fluids and could not do its job without them.

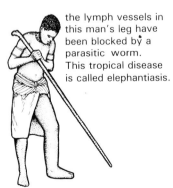

the lymph vessels in this man's leg have been blocked by a parasitic worm. This tropical disease is called elephantiasis.

# Summary and questions

## Summary

The blood system of large, active animals like mammals consists of a pump, blood vessels and blood. The heart is a double pump – half sends blood to the lungs and the other half to the body. Each pump is made up of two parts, the atrium and the more powerful ventricle, with valves to make sure blood doesn't flow backwards. The arteries are large muscular blood vessels leading from the heart, the largest being the aorta. The veins, which have thinner walls, return blood to the heart. Capillaries form a link between arteries and veins. They allow some blood to leak out and, as tissue fluid, to bathe the body cells.

Most tissue fluid soon returns to the capillaries, but some enters the lymph system. This rejoins the blood system at a vein in the neck. In this way the various body fluids form a connected system.

## Questions

1. Match the description with the name. Write out full sentences.

| Name | Description |
|---|---|
| (a) The heart | are tubes leaving the heart. |
| (b) Arteries | is a pump to keep blood moving. |
| (c) Veins | link larger blood vessels. |
| (d) Capillaries | return blood to the heart.. |

2. Draw a diagram of the heart showing the ventricles contracted. Label the following: aorta, vena cava, left atrium, right atrium, left ventricle, right ventricle, pulmonary vein, pulmonary artery, open valves, closed valves.

3. Explain how
   (a) one-way valves in a vein work
   (b) blood vessels control the way organs and tissues in the body get the blood they need
   (c) a double-pump heart (like yours) is more suitable for a large, active animal than a single-pump heart (like a fish's)

4. Make a poster advertising the heart as a pump.

5. If the pacemaker in someone's heart is faulty, as the result of disease, it can sometimes be replaced by an artificial pacemaker which provides small electrical shocks to the heart muscles.
   (a) One kind of artificial pacemaker causes the muscles to contract 70 times a minute. This is about right for normal activities. What problems might a person with one of these have if they wanted to climb mountains or take part in a game of football?
   (b) Some people have problems with the link between the ventricles and the pacemaker (in the atrium), which otherwise works normally. They may be able to have an artificial pacemaker which picks up the natural rhythm of impulses from the tissue in the atrium and passes them on to the ventricles. Why is this kind of artificial pacemaker better than the one in part (a)?

6. What is the importance of the following in the blood system?
   (a) pacemaker
   (b) aorta
   (c) atrium
   (d) coronary artery
   (e) lymph

# Blood cells

## Portrait of a red blood cell

**Shape:** a flattened disc – thinner in the middle. They are flexible for squeezing through capillaries.

**Size:** 125 of them in a line stretch about 1 mm.

**Number:** you might have 25 million million of them.

**Age:** 4 months at most – millions are born and die every day.

**Made in:** bone marrow of adult humans.

**Disposed of:** in the spleen or the liver. Most haemoglobin is recycled (used again).

**Made of:** a membrane bag full of haemoglobin solution. There is no nucleus to leave more room for haemoglobin.

**Job:** haemoglobin picks up oxygen in the lungs, and drops it off in body tissues. Haemoglobin also helps carry carbon dioxide back to the lungs.

**Not enough of them:** you have anaemia. This can be the result of shortage of iron or Vitamin B12, though there are many causes. In any case, the patient is pale and breathless – oxygen is not getting to the tissues fast enough.

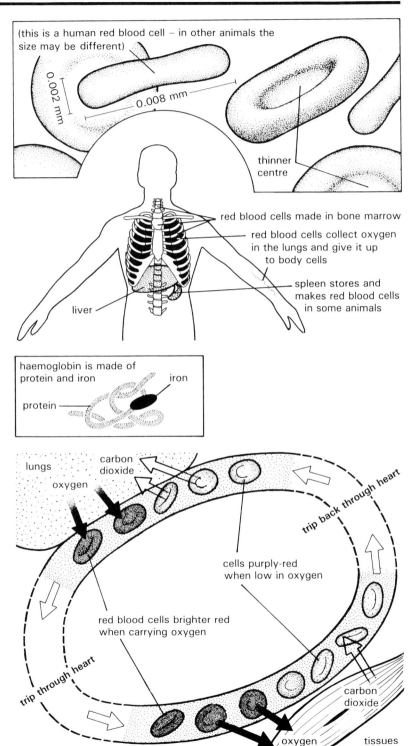

(this is a human red blood cell – in other animals the size may be different)

0.002 mm

0.008 mm

thinner centre

red blood cells made in bone marrow

red blood cells collect oxygen in the lungs and give it up to body cells

spleen stores and makes red blood cells in some animals

liver

haemoglobin is made of protein and iron

iron

protein

lungs

carbon dioxide

oxygen

trip back through heart

cells purply-red when low in oxygen

red blood cells brighter red when carrying oxygen

trip through heart

carbon dioxide

oxygen

tissues

## Portrait of a white blood cell

**Shape:** varies – there are several kinds of white blood cells. They can change shape, and wriggle out of capillaries.

**Size:** varies from the size of a red blood cell to three times the size.

**Number:** about $\frac{1}{700}$ as many as red blood cells.

**Age:** from a few days to several years.

**Made in:** thymus, bone marrow, spleen and lymph system.

**Made of:** membrane, cytoplasm and nucleus, with special abilities.

**Job:** body defence. There are two main groups. Large ones absorb invaders like bacteria. Small ones make antibodies. Antibodies react with the surface of an invader and make it easier to absorb and destroy it.

**When things go wrong.** A person without enough of them has no resistance to disease. Leukaemia happens when white blood cells multiply uncontrollably – so it's a type of cancer. The dividing cells do not become mature white blood cells and do not defend the body.

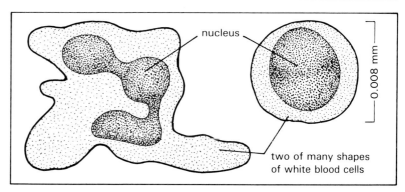

nucleus

0.008 mm

two of many shapes of white blood cells

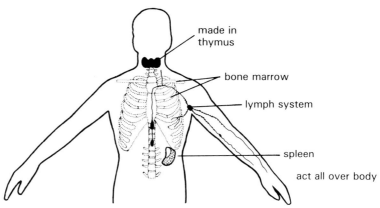

made in thymus

bone marrow

lymph system

spleen

act all over body

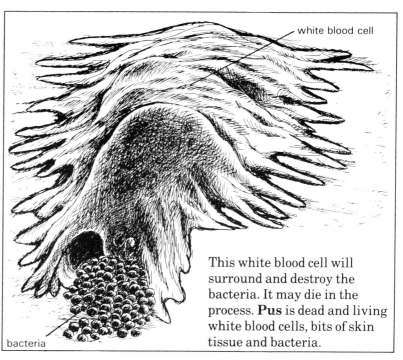

white blood cell

bacteria

This white blood cell will surround and destroy the bacteria. It may die in the process. **Pus** is dead and living white blood cells, bits of skin tissue and bacteria.

# More about blood

## Wound healing

Wounded people sometimes bleed to death, but usually they don't.
The body has an efficient repair system.

Cut blood vessels rapidly constrict. If they are small enough, they
become plugged with blood platelets. A more secure plug is
quickly formed, as shown in the diagrams.

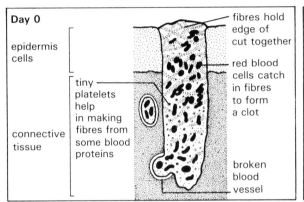

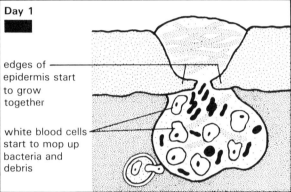

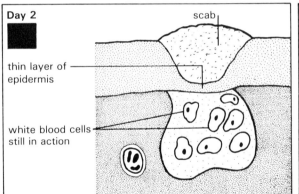

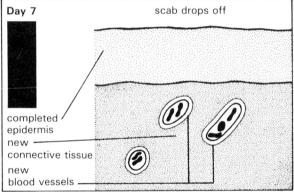

A bruise is the result of blood vessels breaking inside the body,
spilling blood under the skin.

## Problems

Clots are useful as long as they do not spread beyond the area
where they are needed. There is a system of proteins which
breaks up clots, but if it does not keep up with the clotting system
there can be problems. Clotting inside blood vessels –
thrombosis – can be dangerous because clots can block important
blood vessels. In a coronary thrombosis the blood vessels which
supply the heart muscles are blocked. Haemophilia is a rare
disease in which the blood does not clot at all.

## Blood and heat transport

Some animals do not produce much heat. Their body temperature tends to be the same as the temperature of their surroundings. When it's hot they are hot. When it's cold so are they – and they slow down. Other (warm-blooded) animals eat more and make heat from some of the energy in the food. They can keep moving fast all the time, but only if heat is available all over the body.

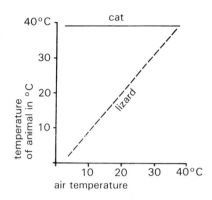

Heat is produced by the liver and muscles. Heat production can be increased when necessary, for example by shivering. Blood spreads the heat around the body.

Control of body temperature involves the blood vessels to the skin, since this is where most heat is lost. The more hot blood there is flowing near the skin surface, the more heat is lost. Muscle cells in the walls of arterioles determine which capillaries the blood flows through.

Warm-blooded animals do not keep the whole of their body at the same temperature. In people the centre of the body is kept steady at about 37°C, but the hands, feet and skin are allowed to be cooler.

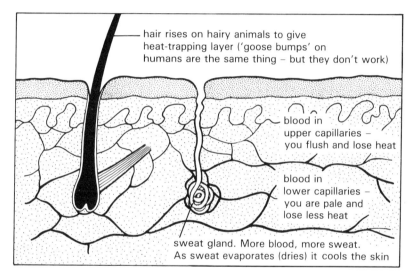

hair rises on hairy animals to give heat-trapping layer ('goose bumps' on humans are the same thing – but they don't work)

blood in upper capillaries – you flush and lose heat

blood in lower capillaries – you are pale and lose less heat

sweat gland. More blood, more sweat. As sweat evaporates (dries) it cools the skin

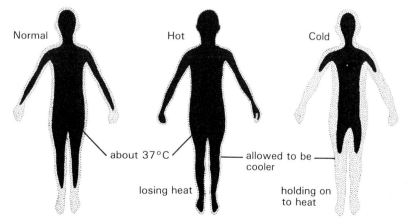

Normal    Hot    Cold

about 37°C

allowed to be cooler

losing heat

holding on to heat

The skin with its blood supply is not the only way organisms control their temperature, but it is very important.

# Transplants

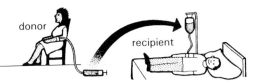

donor
recipient

Replacing a diseased organ by a healthy one seems like a good idea, but transplants are difficult. Even in a simple case – blood transfusions – patients used to die.

In 1900 Karl Landsteiner discovered why – and transfusions became safer. The answer lay in **blood groups**. Your blood group is decided by one or two of the proteins you have in your red blood cells. You may have **antibodies** in your plasma for the red cell proteins you haven't got.

If you mix blood from two similar groups, nothing happens.

If you mix blood with plasma which has the wrong type of antibodies, they clump the red blood cells. The cells are destroyed and capillaries are damaged, as they are blocked by the clumps.

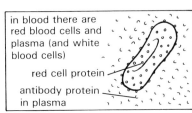

in blood there are red blood cells and plasma (and white blood cells)

red cell protein

antibody protein in plasma

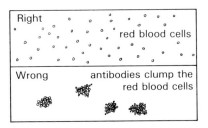

Right
red blood cells

Wrong
antibodies clump the red blood cells

| If your blood group is | you have these red cell proteins | but **not** | and your plasma has these antibodies | these antibodies clump blood cells from | so you can only receive blood from |
|---|---|---|---|---|---|
| A | A | B | anti-B | B and AB people | A and O people |
| B | B | A | anti-A | A and AB people | B and O people |
| O | neither | A and B | anti-A and anti-B | A, B and AB people | O people |
| AB | A and B | neither | neither | nobody | anybody |

Blood cells are soon replaced by the recipient's own cells. Transplants which have to last longer have greater problems.

The small differences in the proteins of the donor and recipient tissues trigger the recipient's defence system. White blood cells normally make antibodies to attack invaders like bacteria. They can also make them against the cells of a transplant. This may take a few days or weeks, and during this time a transplant patient is given treatment to prevent the white blood cells from acting. The patient is defenceless against disease and has to live in near-sterile conditions. Donors are chosen so that chemical differences are as few as possible. At the moment only a few organs, such as kidneys, can be transplanted. Rejection is likely – the recipient's defences destroy the transplant.

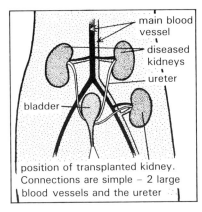

main blood vessel

diseased kidneys

ureter

bladder

position of transplanted kidney. Connections are simple – 2 large blood vessels and the ureter

The cornea is special, as it has no blood supply and is not affected by the defence system. Undamaged corneas can be used to repair damage to the front of the eye. They are taken from people who have given permission for their eyes to be used after death.

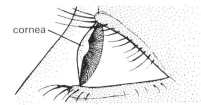

cornea

# Immunization

Once you've had some diseases, you don't catch them again –
you're **immune**. Part of the body defence system which formed to
fight the disease remains ready for action after the disease is
over. The next time they're needed, antibodies form quickly
instead of after several days. The disease organism does not have
a chance to multiply and make you ill.

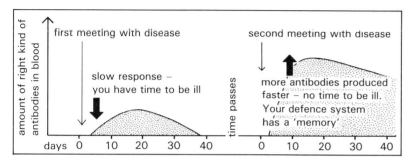

**Immunization** involves giving the body a dose of the
disease-causing organism in weakened or dead form. No illness
results but the defence system is triggered. If an immunized
person later meets the same disease organism the defence system
acts at once – the organism doesn't have a chance.

| **weakened strains can be used to immunize against** | |
| --- | --- |
| smallpox | polio |
| TB | rabies |

| **dead micro-organisms can be used in defence against** | | |
| --- | --- | --- |
| cholera | | flu |
| measles | rabies | polio |

smallpox rash

Immunization doesn't always work, but one big success story is
smallpox – a disease which once killed up to half the people who
caught it. It looks as though a programme of immunization run
by the World Health Organization has wiped out this disease
completely – but only time will make this certain.

It has been a long struggle. The ancient Chinese partly protected
themselves by using a weak strain of smallpox which they
introduced by a scratch in the skin. Edward Jenner improved the
technique in 1796. There was a folk story that people who had
had cowpox, a mild disease caught from cattle, did not catch
smallpox. Jenner tested the idea on a young man – James
Phipps – who did not catch smallpox after the inoculation of
cowpox. The idea eventually caught on after a lot of resistance.
Immunization is also known as vaccination, after Jenner's
discovery. Vaccinus is the Latin word for cow.

Improvements in immunization against smallpox seem to have
been successful, but just one smallpox victim could start an
epidemic. People gradually lose their immunity, and they aren't
having smallpox vaccinations any more.

# Plasma and water

Plasma is mainly water, but dissolved in it are proteins, sugars, salt and lots of other substances. It is important that plasma is of the right concentration. Why?

Look at it from a red blood cell's point of view. Remember osmosis?

This is the normal set-up.

This happens when animals are very dehydrated (dried out). Blood gets thick, and red blood cells can't work properly. Humans are very ill when they lose 1/10 of their body water.

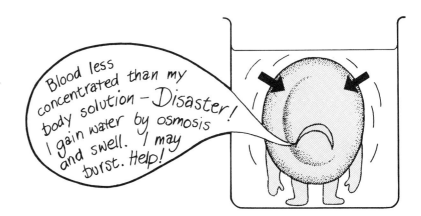

This can happen when an organism is dry and then drinks a lot of water suddenly. Desert animals like camels cope better than people. Their bodies can lose three times more water than ours, and their red blood cells do not burst if they drink a lot of water fast.

# Summary and questions

## Summary

Blood consists of the following:

(a) plasma – a watery solution which transports heat, dissolved food, wastes and gases round the body. It also transports proteins, which include antibodies and some hormones

(b) red blood cells – important in the transport of gases, especially oxygen

(c) white blood cells – involved in defending the body from invaders like bacteria

(d) platelets – which, along with some of the blood proteins, are important in clotting.

Blood must be of the right concentration, otherwise osmosis can damage cells.

## Questions

1. Write this out – filling in the blanks.
   By far the most common of the two types of cells in blood are the _____ blood cells. White blood cells are involved in _____ the body, while red blood cells transport _____ from the _____ to the _____ _____, and transport carbon dioxide back again. _____ blood cells remain in capillaries, but _____ blood cells can leave these vessels. Red blood cells contain _____ made of protein and _____ but have no _____. White blood cells do have a _____, although the shape may be unusual.

2. Draw a diagram of
   (a) a red blood cell
   (b) a white blood cell
   Show how big each cell is. Where are the cells made? Which is likely to live longest?

3. Carbon monoxide is produced by car engines and cigarettes. It reacts with haemoglobin and will not come unstuck (unlike $CO_2$ or $O_2$). Once this has happened, the haemoglobin is no good for transporting other things. What do you think would happen to a person who had breathed in (i) a little carbon monoxide (ii) a lot of carbon monoxide? Why?

4. How is blood involved in keeping a mammal's body at a steady temperature? Write a limerick beginning
   'There was a young reindeer called . . .'
   as part of your answer.

5. (a) Animals like frogs are often described as cold-blooded. Why do you think this is misleading?
   (b) In very cold conditions, people sometimes lose fingers or toes because the blood supply has been cut off for so long (frostbite). This isn't too great, but the alternative is worse. What is the alternative and why is it worse?
   (c) James Bond staggers out of the desert. He has walked many miles in the blazing heat. He begs for a drink – a big drink – of water. Do you give him lots of water or a little? Why?

6. Dave cuts himself and the blood spurts out in bright scarlet bursts. Pete cuts himself, but the blood is darker and flows out smoothly. (Both have cut their arms.)
   (a) One of them has cut through an artery and one a vein. Who has done what? Explain your answer.
   (b) You want to reduce bleeding enough to give the clotting mechanisms a chance to work. You take different kinds of action in the two cases. Which of the following methods would you use in Pete's case? Why?
   (i) See if you can find a pressure point between the wound and the heart where the blood vessel can be flattened against a bone. Press there.
   (ii) Raise the limb in the air.
   (c) Briefly describe what happens once bleeding has slowed enough for clotting to start.

# Water cycle

Water – like other materials vital to organisms – circulates endlessly between living things and the environment.

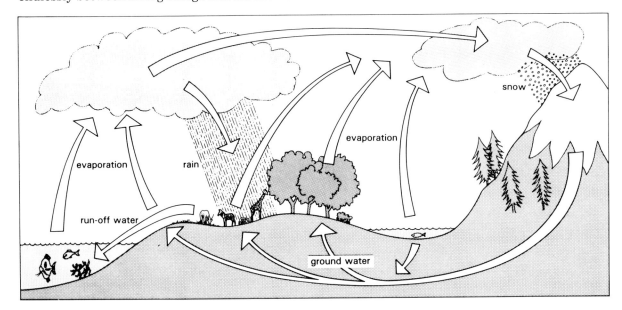

All living things need water. In the water cycle, only some water passes through living things. Aquatic plants have no trouble but land plants may have problems getting enough water.

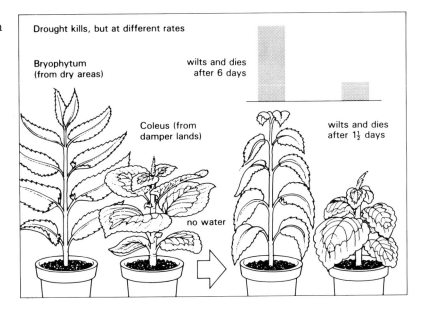

The amount of water available is very important in deciding what plants grow where. All land plants have ways of holding on to water, but those in dry areas do it particularly well.

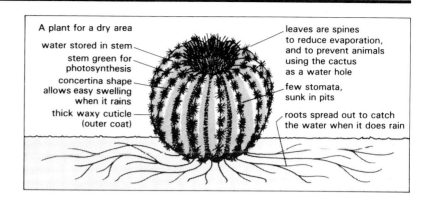

A plant for a dry area

water stored in stem

stem green for photosynthesis

concertina shape allows easy swelling when it rains

thick waxy cuticle (outer coat)

leaves are spines to reduce evaporation, and to prevent animals using the cactus as a water hole

few stomata, sunk in pits

roots spread out to catch the water when it does rain

In general an organism must gain each day the amount of water it loses. (Growing organisms need extra water, as they need extra everything else). The diagram shows a possible water balance for a human for one day. Your water balance is probably different. Your size, the air temperature and how much you drink are just a few of the sources of variation.

drink 1200 cm³

in food 500 cm³

from chemical reactions 400 cm³

through lungs 500 cm³

skin 500 cm³

gut 100 cm³

kidneys 1000 cm³

gained

lost

add them up to check the balance

The kidneys are important in varying water loss. They are also important in animals which have to get rid of extra water. Fresh-water fish have blood more concentrated than pond or river or lake water.

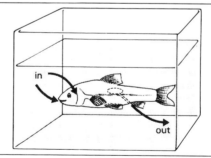

in

out

Water enters by osmosis. Kidneys get rid of extra water as urine – otherwise fish would swell.

However, kidneys can cause problems. Salt-water fish have blood less concentrated than sea water.

They lose water by osmosis. They also lose some through the kidneys, though they only produce enough urine to get rid of wastes.

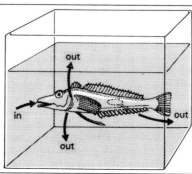

out

in

out

out

These fish drink salt water and pump the salt out through the gills. The left-over water makes up for losses.

We live on land, where water loss is always a problem – so why do we have kidneys, and how do they work? Read on to find out.

The cells of an animal's body live in water, whether the animal does or not. Regardless of what the animal eats, the cells must have a stable environment – maintained (in mammals) mainly by the kidneys. Kidneys do three things at once.

(a) they control the amount of water in the body
(b) they control the amount of salt and other minerals in the body
(c) they excrete (get rid of) urea and other wastes containing nitrogen.

Kidneys produce a concentrated urea solution, called **urine** (pee), which trickles down tubes to the bladder for short-term storage.

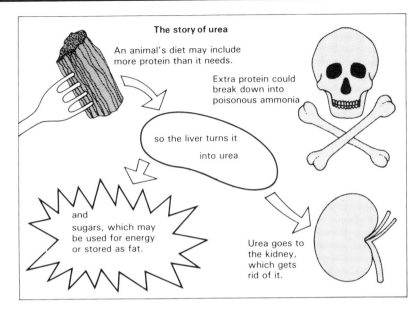

The story of urea

An animal's diet may include more protein than it needs.

Extra protein could break down into poisonous ammonia

so the liver turns it into urea

and sugars, which may be used for energy or stored as fat.

Urea goes to the kidney, which gets rid of it.

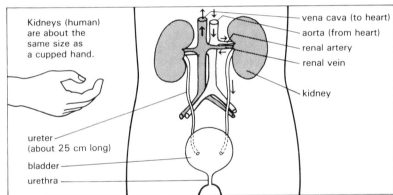

Kidneys (human) are about the same size as a cupped hand.

vena cava (to heart)
aorta (from heart)
renal artery
renal vein
kidney

ureter (about 25 cm long)
bladder
urethra

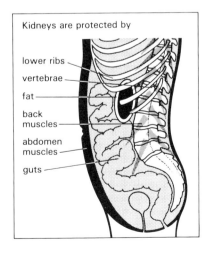

Kidneys are protected by

lower ribs
vertebrae
fat
back muscles
abdomen muscles
guts

Kidneys are fragile, but one normally functioning kidney is enough to keep the body healthy.

Cut in half, a kidney is dark red. A lot of blood flows through it and is processed by it – 70 litres an hour.

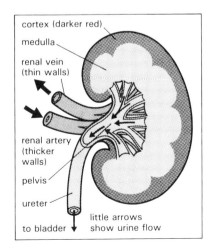

cortex (darker red)
medulla
renal vein (thin walls)
renal artery (thicker walls)
pelvis
ureter
to bladder
little arrows show urine flow

Under a microscope, the medulla and cortex are a confusing mass of tubes. These tubes are capillaries plus the kidney tubules – **nephrons**.

Straightened out, each nephron would be 40 mm long.

They are *very* thin. Each kidney contains about a million nephrons.

Each nephron is folded up.

nephron

cortex is dark red – contains lots of blood

closed end – the Bowman's capsule

40 mm

liquid

open end of tube leads into collecting duct to pelvis

The Bowman's capsule surrounds a knot of blood capillaries – the **glomerulus**. Blood pressure forces water and smaller molecules into the nephron.

Start of a nephron

some plasma, plus proteins and red blood cells

water

urea

whole blood

glomerulus

Bowman's capsule

glucose

salt

to rest of nephron

As the liquid moves through the nephron, tubule cells collect useful items – glucose, most of the salt and minerals, and water. These are returned to the blood. Capillaries wind around the tubule.

The tubule cells can vary the amount of salt and water they retrieve.
Drinking a lot results in lots of dilute urine, because the tubules take back less water.
If there is too much salt in food, the tubules take less salt back into the blood.
A water shortage means a smaller amount of more concentrated urine, as the body holds on to its water.
In any case, the body gets rid of its urea (though some urea may take several trips through the kidney before it is removed).
This diagram just shows what happens, not what it looks like.

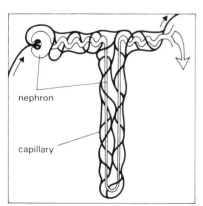

nephron

capillary

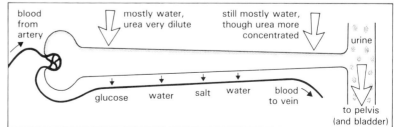

blood from artery

mostly water, urea very dilute

still mostly water, though urea more concentrated

urine

glucose    water    salt    water    blood to vein

to pelvis (and bladder)

# Other wastes

Organisms produce a number of unwanted materials as part of their body chemistry. Getting rid of them (and getting rid of excess materials taken in) is called **excretion**.

**Plants** have few excretion problems. They tick over more slowly than animals, and wastes build up slowly. Unlike animals they can

(a) re-use waste nitrogenous materials
(b) use up the waste product of respiration ($CO_2$) in photosynthesis.

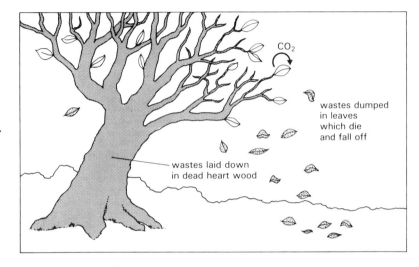

CO₂

wastes dumped in leaves which die and fall off

wastes laid down in dead heart wood

In **animals,** excretion involves getting rid of a number of waste materials. The diagram shows the routes used by mammals.

**liver**
some poisons and drugs
bile (cholesterol plus parts of old red blood cells)

**lungs**
water
carbon dioxide

**skin**
water
salts

**kidneys**
water
urea
salts

## N.B.

Undigested food leaving as faeces doesn't count in excretion, as it has never been part of the body – just passing through.

# Summary and questions

## Summary
A final round-up on water, which is recycled by organisms and the environment all the time. The water balance of an organism is always important and the kidney is especially vital in providing a suitable concentration of body fluids to bathe cells. The kidney is also important in getting rid of nitrogen waste in the form of urea made by the liver. Urea and water and a little salt form urine which is excreted. The excretion of other wastes often involves the same organs as water loss.

## Questions

1. Write this out in full – filling in the blanks. There are _____ kidneys, one on each side of the body. They are protected by _____ and _____ _____ and _____. They make a liquid called _____ which is mostly _____ and _____. This liquid runs down two tubes called _____ to the _____ where it is stored for a while. Kidneys are well supplied with _____ which arrives at the rate of 70 _____ an hour from the _____ artery. Most of it returns to the general circulation via the _____ _____.

2. What is meant by the following?
   (a) water cycle
   (b) wilting
   (c) osmosis
   (d) nephron
   (e) excretion
   Diagrams may be helpful.

3. Skin is important in excretion and many other processes. Make your own summary – look up all the references to skin in *Biology for You 1* and *2* (you'll have to use the index). Make notes and then write and draw your own double-page spread. Include diagrams, and try to explain how skin is suited to doing the jobs it does.

4. Give as detailed an answer as you can when you explain the difference between each of the following pairs:
   (a) run-off water and ground water
   (b) ureter and urethra
   (c) renal vein and renal artery
   (d) Bowman's capsule and a glomerulus

5. (a) Water moves in and out of a fish through the gut lining and the gills. Why not the rest of the fish's surface?
   (b) How much water is gained and lost by a human each day, according to the text? (It's just an average.)
   (c) What would probably happen to the amount of urine produced if a person (i) drank six large cups of tea? (ii) lay all day in the sun without drinking any extra liquid? (iii) drank just over a litre of liquid during the day? (iv) ate several large slices of water melon?
   (d) Why do you think the text says that cells live in water?

6. (a) Draw a diagram of the outside of a kidney.
   (b) Label the tubes to it and from it.
   (c) Say what the tubes contain and how the contents differ from each other.

7. It is very difficult to feel a person's kidneys from the outside unless the person is very thin. Explain why this is so.

8. Make four suggestions about how an animal living in the desert could reduce the problem of water loss. (Hint – look at the ways water is lost from a mammal's body. Look at ways desert plants reduce water loss. Think about behaviour patterns and what you do when it is very hot. Read up about animals like the camel – which stores fat, not water, in its hump.)

# Adaptation

Organisms fit well into the world in which we live. They survive because their body structure, the way their bodies work and their behaviour are suited to coping with the problems of living in their environment. There have been many examples of adaptation in *Biology for You* so far.

Adaptations allow cacti to use what water there is and protect them against heat and drought. Sometimes rather different organisms solve the problems in similar ways – they have similar adaptations.

## Solving movement problems

### (a) Adaptations for moving in air

They all have light bones which support a large surface.

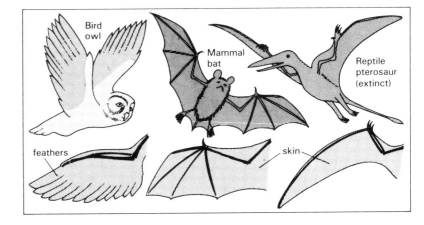

### (b) Adaptations for moving in water

They all have a streamlined shape and use limbs as paddles.

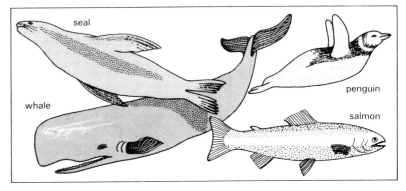

Related organisms can have adaptations for different ways of life.

**Beaks adapted to eating different foods**

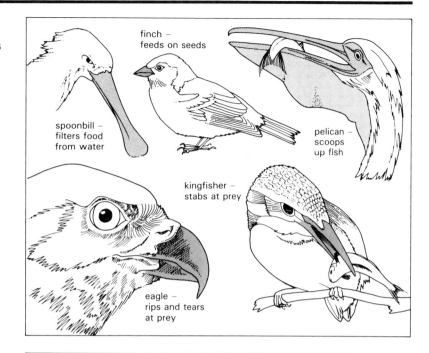

How do they (and we) get to be like that? Much of the rest of this book tries to answer this quesion – and explain why some possibilities don't happen.

# Parasites

Parasites are organisms which live on or in another organism – the host. (They include some worms, single-celled organisms, fungi, and many more.) It is a one-sided relationship. The host provides food (and shelter) and in return is damaged by the parasite.

The host loses blood. The parasite may carry disease, and it makes holes where bacteria can attack.

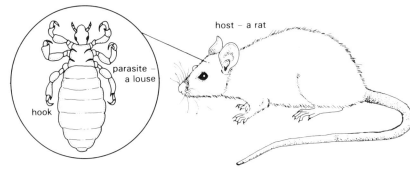

A well-adapted parasite does not do too much damage, though. It is not a good idea to kill the host that feeds you.

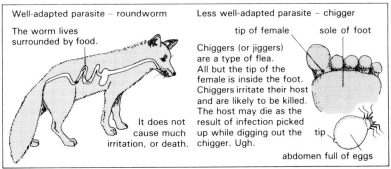

Well-adapted parasite – roundworm

The worm lives surrounded by food.

It does not cause much irritation, or death.

Less well-adapted parasite – chigger

tip of female     sole of foot

Chiggers (or jiggers) are a type of flea. All but the tip of the female is inside the foot. Chiggers irritate their host and are likely to be killed. The host may die as the result of infection picked up while digging out the chigger. Ugh.

tip

abdomen full of eggs

The adaptations of a parasite depend upon where it lives. Many can only survive in one place in one kind of host.

**For example:** large roundworms are common in the guts of people all over the world. Their eggs leave the body in faeces. If the eggs get into drinking water or on dirty hands they can be swallowed, and so start life in a new host. Infection is very likely if sewage treatment is poor or absent.

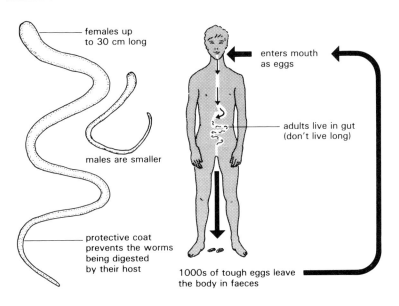

females up to 30 cm long

males are smaller

protective coat prevents the worms being digested by their host

enters mouth as eggs

adults live in gut (don't live long)

1000s of tough eggs leave the body in faeces

Some gut-living worms have extra adaptations. Tapeworms have hooks and suckers at the head end of their ribbon-like bodies to hold on to the gut wall. The rest of the body is an egg-making machine. Who needs a gut in a food-filled environment?

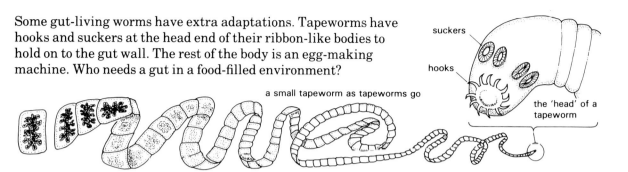

a small tapeworm as tapeworms go

suckers

hooks

the 'head' of a tapeworm

Tapeworms have an extra step in their life cycle, which helps them to find new hosts. They produce many eggs, a few of which are eaten by a secondary host. The eggs develop into bladder worms in the muscles of the secondary host. If the muscles (meat) are eaten raw or undercooked, the bladder worms survive and develop into adult tapeworms in the gut. (Have you ever eaten a rare steak?)

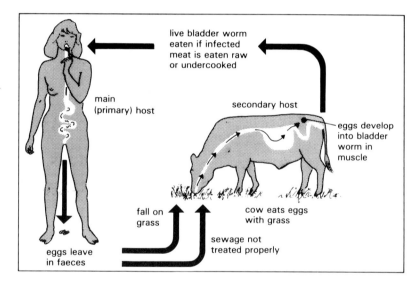

live bladder worm eaten if infected meat is eaten raw or undercooked

main (primary) host

secondary host

eggs develop into bladder worm in muscle

cow eats eggs with grass

fall on grass

sewage not treated properly

eggs leave in faeces

Some tapeworms have fish, pigs or dogs as secondary hosts.

Parasites gnaw into other parts of the body and often do a lot of damage. They may live in blood, lymph, muscles, brains and so on. Adaptations include ways of fooling the host's white blood cells – and solving the transport problem.

The blood sucked up by this mosquito might contain malaria parasites – hitching a lift to the blood of a new host.

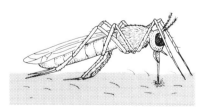

Adult parasites often seem very dull. They sit there, feeding through their skin and reproducing. They haven't got much in the way of a nervous system, or means of moving, or sense organs. *But* they have a successful way of life – there are probably more of them than of all other types of organisms put together.

# Variety

Organisms show lots of variety in their adaptations. There are many types of plants and animals.

There is variety among organisms of the same species.

There is even variety among parts of the same organism.

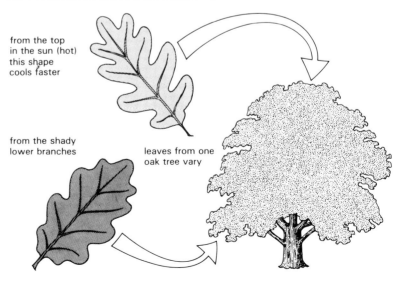

from the top in the sun (hot) this shape cools faster

from the shady lower branches

leaves from one oak tree vary

New adaptations are based on variety which already exists. It looks as though organisms pass on to their children the variety they **inherited** from their parents.

docked (cut) tail

The pups' ears will prick up like the parents' ears when they are older. Their tails will stay long unless they are cut.

It can be hard to sort out how much of the variety is due to the effect of the **environment** on an organism, and how much is inherited. Experiments can help.

well fed    underfed

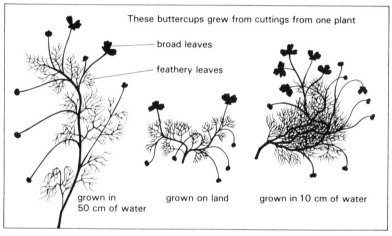

These buttercups grew from cuttings from one plant

broad leaves

feathery leaves

grown in 50 cm of water    grown on land    grown in 10 cm of water

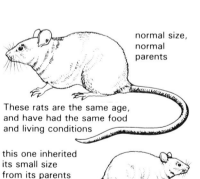

normal size, normal parents

These rats are the same age, and have had the same food and living conditions

this one inherited its small size from its parents

It is sometimes possible to show how much of the differences between organisms is due to inheritance.

However, it isn't always possible to tell – real life is complicated.

Try this problem on your friends. Do they all take the same time to do it?

Do you get your intelligence from the way you are brought up? or inherit it from your parents? or both? Nobody is sure.

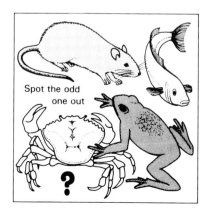

Spot the odd one out

?

# Sex and variety

Being able to reproduce is an important feature of living things. They can do it in two quite different ways, and these give different amounts of variety in the offspring.

**Sexual reproduction** involves the meeting of two sex cells – a sperm and an egg. Watch out for:

flowers which can be male or female or both,

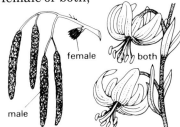

and animals with a male and female.

More about this later.

**Asexual reproduction** is reproduction without sex. It involves only one parent and no sex cells. It has advantages – offspring get a good start in life, since they are fed by the parent for quite a long time. On the rest of this page are some examples.
Some plants send out runners. Potatoes reproduce asexually. 'Spuds' are tubers – the swollen ends of underground stems. Plant a tuber and it'll grow into a new potato plant. Some plants reproduce by budding. So do some animals. The buds break away. Some organisms reproduce both sexually and asexually.

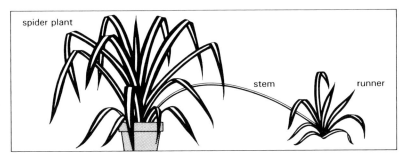

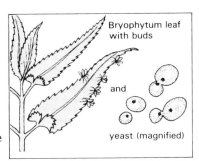

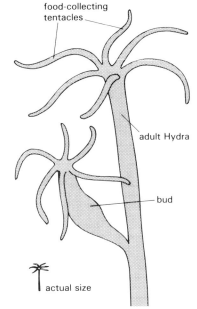

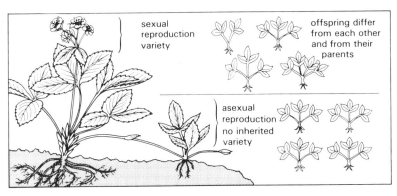

Hydra lives in water and is related to jellyfish and coral.

# Summary and questions

**Summary**
Organisms are adapted – suited – to their environment. It depends upon the problems to be solved in each way of life. A parasite which lives on or in a larger organism, the host, is an example of extreme adaptation. It cannot survive in any other way. In finding out how organisms become adapted, we begin by noting that organisms vary a lot. At least some of the variety is inherited from parents. Some variety is the result of the effect of the environment on an organism. To some extent the amount of variety in a group of organisms depends on the way they reproduce. Sexual reproduction produces more varied offspring than asexual (non-sexual) reproduction.

**Questions**

1. Give the number of adaptations each question asks for, and explain how they work.
   (a) three adaptations which allow plants to survive heat and drought
   (b) two adaptations for flight
   (c) two adaptations for swimming
   (d) one adaptation of a louse for life as a parasite
   (e) two adaptations of a tapeworm for life as a parasite
   (f) one way buttercup leaves adapt for life under water
   (g) one way oak leaves adapt for their position on an oak tree

2. Adaptation sometimes refers to individuals and the way they change in reaction to their environment. You adapt to cold by shivering, eating more heat-providing food, and so on. In question 1, two of the examples are of this kind of adaptation. Which? How do you adapt to    (a) high temperatures, (b) drinking too much    (c) invasion by harmful bacteria?

3. Which of the following do you think are inherited, and which are the result of the environment acting on an organism? Why?
   (a) the pricked ears of a boxer dog
   (b) the short tail of a boxer dog
   (c) a person's eye colour
   (d) the length of a person's hair
   (e) the fat stomach of a cat whose owner feeds it chocolate (among other things)

4. Which of the following are acting as parasites? Give a reason for your answer.
   (a) a lion eating an antelope
   (b) a vampire bat drinking the blood of a sleeping donkey
   (c) mistletoe absorbing water and minerals from the sap of an oak tree
   (d) a worm which lives in lymph vessels and causes elephantiasis
   (e) a man drinking milk
   (f) bacteria living in a rabbit's gut and digesting cellulose

5. Wherever there are pairs of brackets, cross out the one which isn't true. Write out what's left. The first one is done for you.

   Parasites live (on)(on or in) an organism (larger)(smaller) than they are. They (damage)(always kill) this organism, which is known as the (prey)(host). One problem is finding new (prey)(hosts). Most parasites living inside the (prey)(host) produce (many)(few) eggs which leave (in faeces only)(in faeces or through the skin). (Many)(few) eggs die, but some enter new (prey)(hosts) through (one of several routes)(the mouth). Some parasites have a (friend)(secondary host) in their life cycle, for example the (tapeworm)(roundworm). A (gut)(blood) parasite has (legs)(protective skin) to prevent it being (respired)(digested). Many parasites living (inside)(outside) the body lose (sense)(reproductive) organs which they no longer need. Parasites may lead a very narrow life, but as a group they are very (unsuccessful)(successful).

# Sexual reproduction in plants

Sexual reproduction is all about two sex cells or **gametes** meeting and fusing. The actual moment when the cells join (**fertilization**) tends to get lost in the preparations and results, even in plants. Still, it's what all the fuss is about.

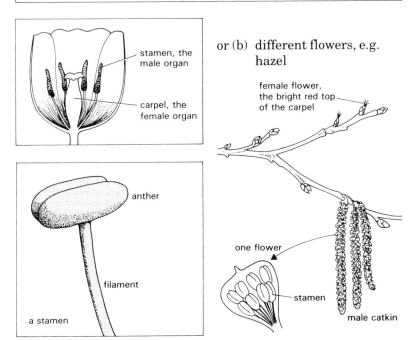

Gametes are made in reproductive organs, which may be
(a) part of the same flower e.g. tulip

stamen, the male organ

carpel, the female organ

or (b) different flowers, e.g. hazel

female flower, the bright red top of the carpel

**Stamens** consist of an **anther** and a **filament**

anther

filament

a stamen

one flower

stamen

male catkin

Pollen is made in the anther, which splits open when ripe to release the dust-like pollen. Pollen coats are very tough. By looking closely at a grain of pollen (an electron microscope is best) you can tell which type of plant it came from.

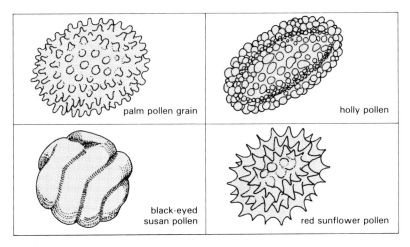

palm pollen grain

holly pollen

black-eyed susan pollen

red sunflower pollen

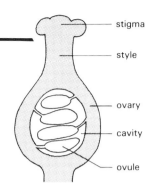

**Carpels** consist of a **stigma**, a **style**, an **ovary** and one or many **ovules**, arranged in various ways. All the parts come in a lot of different shapes and sizes. The stigma is often sticky to hold pollen.

# Problem

getting pollen to the ovule. Plants have come up with so many solutions that they have a double-page spread to themselves – 'More on pollination', over the page.

Once the pollen grain has arrived on the stigma it splits and a tube starts to grow down through the stigma and style. The pollen tube only grows well if the pollen is from the same kind of plant as the carpel.

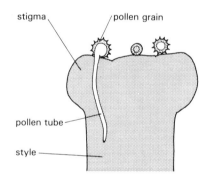

When it reaches the ovary, the pollen tube grows towards an ovule and enters it. It is hard to see what happens in fertilization, but it seems that the tip of the tube breaks and a nucleus from the pollen tube meets a nucleus in the ovule and joins up with it.

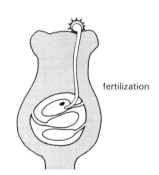

The ex-ovule grows into a seed – an embryo plus its food supply. Stamens and petals die. The ovary grows to form a fruit, and the top of the flower stalk may also be involved in helping the seed travel from the parent plant and survive.

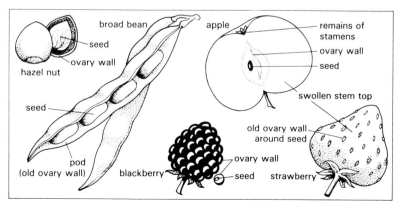

# More on pollination

There are all sorts of methods of transporting pollen from stamen to stigma. Flowers are usually adapted to one way or another. Pollen travels by **water** in a few plants like Canadian pond weed. There are more kinds of plants whose pollen travel by **wind** – examples include nettles, dock, trees with catkins, oaks and grasses.

Watch out for:

1. large amounts of small light pollen
2. small scentless flowers, often green
3. feathery stigmas – they have large surfaces to catch pollen
4. large anthers hanging out on long filaments so that pollen is easily blown away
5. flowers held above leaves or produced before leaves are out.

rye grass

feathery stigma

large anther

**Animal pollination** is also common. The flowers are quite different. They attract animals which carry pollen from flower to flower on their bodies.

(a) The flower provides something the animals want – usually food, such as extra **pollen** to eat or **nectar** to drink. Nectar is a sugary liquid which animals like bees turn into honey.

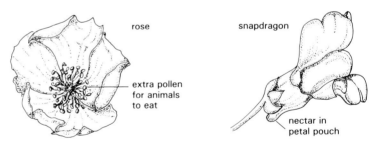

rose

extra pollen for animals to eat

snapdragon

nectar in petal pouch

(b) The flower signals to the animals. It pays to advertise!

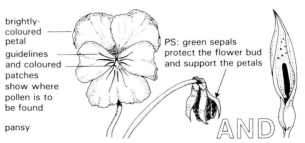

brightly-coloured petal

guidelines and coloured patches show where pollen is to be found

pansy

PS: green sepals protect the flower bud and support the petals

AND

Scents, not always nice, attract pollinators. Cuckoo pint smells rather like dung to attract flies which lay eggs in cow pats.

cuckoo pint

(c) The flower is constructed so that as an animal collects food, it brushes against the stigma and stamens. This means it picks up pollen, and pollen already on it from another flower rubs off.

Fuschias are pollinated by humming-birds in South America.

stamens

stigma

In the UK, only bumble bees are big enough.

Butterflies spread pollen as they walk across Buddleia.

stamen

stigma

nectar

bindweed

honeysuckle

A hawk moth collects pollen on its head as it pushes its proboscis into the petal tube.

In all the flowers we have seen so far, pollen travels from one flower to another, often on a different plant. This is called **cross-pollination.** **Self-pollination** happens when pollen from the stamens fertilizes an ovule in the same flower. This is less chancey but it reduces variety, and many plants have ways of avoiding it. For example, in rose-bay willowherb, stamens and carpels are not ripe together, so self-fertilization is avoided.

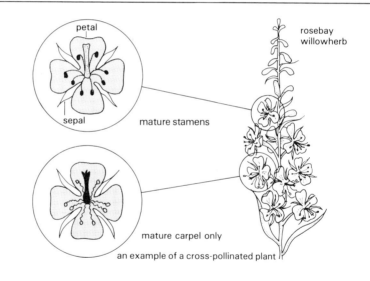

petal

sepal

mature stamens

mature carpel only

an example of a cross-pollinated plant

rosebay willowherb

In some plants, pollen will not grow on the stigma of the flower that produced it. This is self-sterility. Broad beans and peas have lost their self-sterility, and they often self-pollinate. Other plants self-fertilize when there are few insects around to carry their pollen.

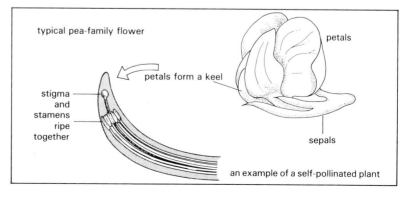

typical pea-family flower

petals form a keel

stigma and stamens ripe together

petals

sepals

an example of a self-pollinated plant

# Plant reproduction and people

Plant reproduction is very important to us – we eat seeds and fruits and organs of vegetative reproduction (like potatoes). We can control pollination to produce new varieties of plants. We often use asexual reproduction to grow more identical plants when we have a useful variety. Here are a few examples.

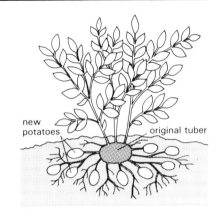

new potatoes    original tuber

The cucumbers we eat are from unpollinated flowers – fertilized seeds produce bitter cucumbers. Bananas don't have fertilized seeds in them either. New banana plants grow from suckers, like strawberry plants.

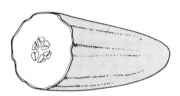

We grow potato plants from potato tubers, not from potato seeds – which would grow into plants different from the parent.

Grafting is used with fruit trees, vines and others to combine different root and shoot systems. A variety with poor fruit but tough roots can be joined to one which has small roots but sweet fruit, to get an ideal combination (from our point of view).

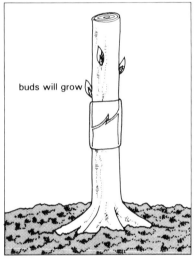

buds will grow

Breeding new plant varieties is fiddly but profitable – more beautiful flowers are worth money. Pansies are a result of cross-breeding three types of violet.

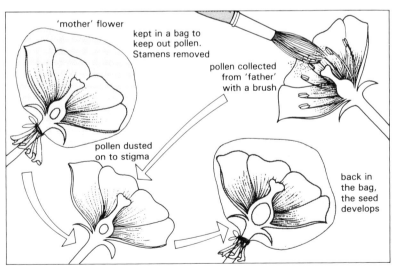

'mother' flower

kept in a bag to keep out pollen. Stamens removed

pollen collected from 'father' with a brush

pollen dusted on to stigma

back in the bag, the seed develops

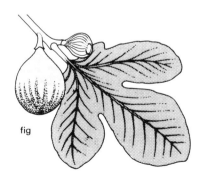

fig

Plants from many parts of the world can grow in Britain, but they may not be able to breed here. They may only be pollinated by one insect, which isn't found in Britain. The fig is an example.

# Summary and questions

## Summary

Flowers are organs of sexual reproduction. They consist of stamens, which are male and make pollen, and carpels which are female and contain ovules or egg cells in an ovary. Carpels also have a stigma, and a style which joins ovary and stigma. Pollination is the transfer of pollen from stamen to stigma. It is usually the result of wind blowing the pollen, or of animals, especially insects, carrying pollen on their bodies. Once on the stigma, pollen grows a pollen tube down to an ovule. Fertilization occurs when pollen and ovule join and form a seed. Flowers also have petals which may be brightly coloured to attract insects. They have an outer layer of sepals (usually green) which protect the delicate bud, and later often support the petals.

## Questions

1. Match up the part of the flower from column A with what it does in column B. Write out complete sentences.

| A | B |
|---|---|
| The anther | is the part of the carpel which receives pollen. |
| The filament | protect buds and support petals. |
| The stigma | is the part of the stamen which makes pollen. |
| The style | may help to attract insects. |
| The ovary | holds up the stigma. |
| Petals | holds up the anther. |
| Sepals | is the part of the carpel which contains the ovule. |

2. Copy out this diagram. Draw it large enough to fill half a page. Label everything which has an arrow pointing to it.

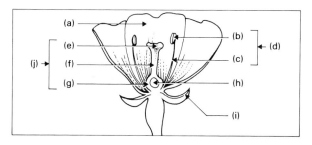

3. This table compares wind-pollinated and animal-pollinated flowers. Fill in the gaps.

| | Wind-pollinated | Animal-pollinated |
|---|---|---|
| pollen is | | small and often sticky |
| the amount of pollen produced is | even larger than in animal-pollinated flowers | large |
| petals are | small and green | |
| scent is | | |
| nectar is | not made | |
| stamens are | | various sizes and shapes. They are often held up |
| stigmas are | often feathery, with a large surface to catch pollen | |
| an example is | | a rose |

4. Make an advertisement for a flower of your choice (or design an ideal flower). The advertisement should bring out why your flower is so good at getting pollinated.

# Sexual reproduction in animals

Sexual activity in animals, as in plants, is aimed at fertilization –
bringing together male and female sex cells or gametes to
produce a cell which can grow into a new organism.

### Sperm – male gametes

Sperm travel. They are small – you need a microscope to see
them. They have tails which thrash around to move them along.
They are produced in large numbers as many do not survive or
are lost.

Sperm vary in shape and
size – but not much.

Much enlarged, a sperm has
three main sections.

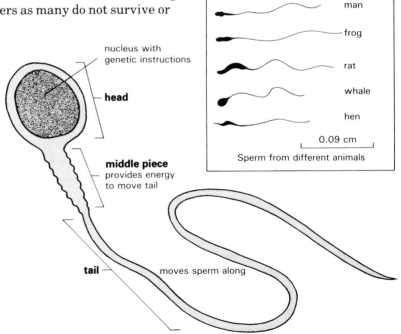

nucleus with
genetic instructions

**head**

**middle piece**
provides energy
to move tail

**tail** — moves sperm along

snake

man

frog

rat

whale

hen

0.09 cm

Sperm from different animals

### Eggs – female gametes

Eggs contain food to start the embryo off in life. They are much larger, don't move, and are produced in smaller numbers.

Unlike sperm, eggs vary in size – to some extent it depends on whether the embryo develops outside the body or not (see Book 1).

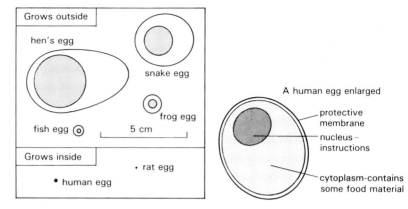

The place where an embryo develops does not have to be the same as the place where fertilization happens. There are three variations.

| Fertilization | Embryo grows | Example | |
|---|---|---|---|
| outside | outside | and fish | **must** have water for reproduction |
| inside | outside | and birds, reptiles, butterflies and so on | doesn't need water. Unless there is a lot of parental care, most eggs get eaten |
| inside | inside | really just mammals, and the odd fish and snake. Do hedgehogs do it? Yes, but very carefully with flattened spines | protection in the womb during early development gives the embryo a good start in life |

Animals have developed interesting mechanisms to improve their chances of reproducing successfully.

# Male reproductive system

The male reproductive organs are for making sperm and getting them into the female. The most noticeable bits of the apparatus are the **penis** (in Latin it means sword) and the **scrotum**, a rather wrinkled skin bag containing the **testes** where sperm and male hormones are made. In many animals the penis is protected inside the body when not in use, but most keep their testes hanging below them where it is cool. Sperm soon die at normal body temperatures.

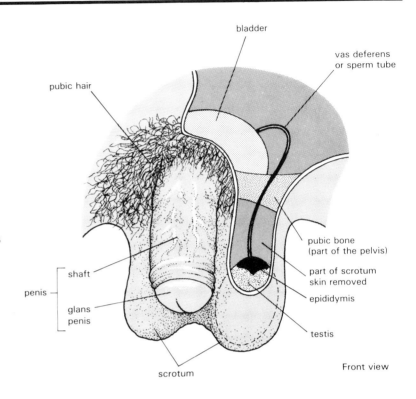

Front view

Inside the testis are many coiled tubules which join up to form the epididymis. This opens into the vas deferens or sperm tube. The walls of the tubules are lined with cells which divide and become sperm at a rate of 50 000 a minute. From here it may take sperm 3 weeks to reach the vas deferens, as the main tube of the epididymis is 6 metres long in man.

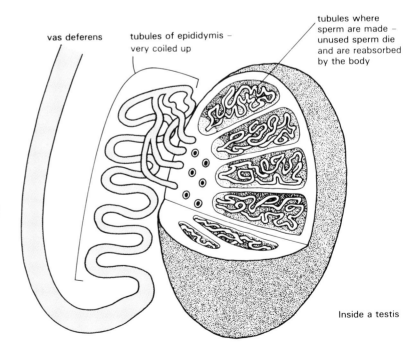

Inside a testis

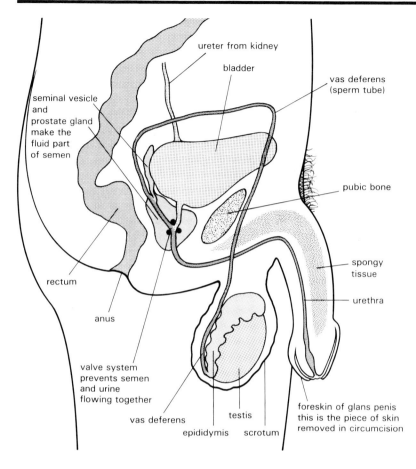

ureter from kidney

bladder

vas deferens
(sperm tube)

seminal vesicle
and
prostate gland
make the
fluid part
of semen

pubic bone

rectum

spongy
tissue

urethra

anus

valve system
prevents semen
and urine
flowing together

vas deferens

testis

foreskin of glans penis
this is the piece of skin
removed in circumcision

epididymis    scrotum

The route of the 400 million or
so sperm which are released
each time a man ejaculates
(comes, has an orgasm) is
easier to follow in a side view.

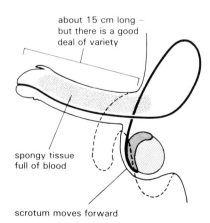

An erect penis

about 15 cm long –
but there is a good
deal of variety

spongy tissue
full of blood

scrotum moves forward

A limp penis is not much use for getting sperm into a female.
Aroused by touch, sight, even imagination, the penis stiffens and
increases in size as blood pours into the spongy tissue faster than
it leaves. Further stimulation results in an ejaculation when the
sticky white semen leaves the penis. Semen is only one-tenth
sperm – the rest is liquid made by the seminal vesicles and
prostate glands. Its job is to provide food and protection for the
sperm. Man normally produces an amount between 0.5 cm$^3$ and
6 cm$^3$ in one ejaculation.

At orgasm, the muscles of the various tubes and the pelvis
contract together and force out semen. Afterwards the penis goes
limp as blood flows out of the spongy tissue.

In animals other than man there are some interesting variations
on the penis – fold-up ones (bulls), penises with bones inside
(sea-lions), long ones (hedgehogs), penises with spines (cats),
forked ones (kangaroos) and so on.

# Female reproductive system

In mammals, the female reproductive organs produce eggs (the female gametes) and provide a safe place for the early growth of offspring (Book 1). Most of the organs are protected inside the body. The few parts you can see are involved in making sure the penis ends up in the right place.

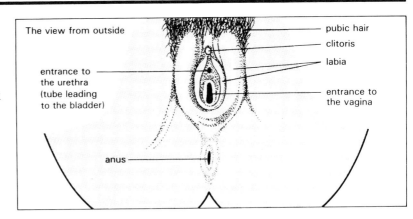

The view from outside

pubic hair
clitoris
labia
entrance to the urethra (tube leading to the bladder)
entrance to the vagina
anus

The **clitoris** has many nerves and is very sensitive. It is usually rubbing the clitoris which causes female orgasm.
The **labia** are flaps which fill up with blood and swell a little. They help guide the penis.
The **vagina** is a muscular tube. When a woman is sexually excited the muscles relax (to fit the penis) and the vagina is lubricated with fluid. During orgasm the vaginal muscles gently relax and contract round the penis.

Inside the body are the **ovaries** where eggs (and sex hormones) are produced and the **uterus** where the embryo grows.

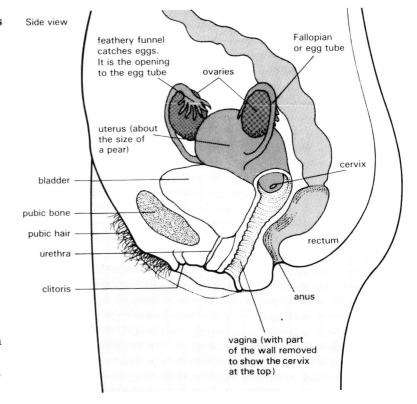

Side view

feathery funnel catches eggs. It is the opening to the egg tube
Fallopian or egg tube
ovaries
uterus (about the size of a pear)
cervix
bladder
pubic bone
pubic hair
urethra
clitoris
rectum
anus
vagina (with part of the wall removed to show the cervix at the top)

The ovaries, unlike the testes, produce very few gametes. Usually one egg is released each month in women between 10 and 50 – though this varies a lot. A woman produces about 400 mature eggs in a lifetime.

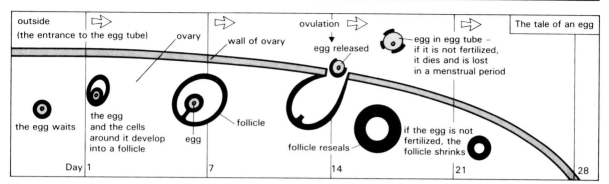

outside
(the entrance to the egg tube)
ovary
wall of ovary
ovulation
egg released
egg in egg tube –
if it is not fertilized,
it dies and is lost
in a menstrual period

the egg waits
the egg
and the cells
around it develop
into a follicle
egg
follicle
follicle reseals
if the egg is not
fertilized, the
follicle shrinks

Day 1    7    14    21    28

To avoid wasting eggs, each month the uterus is prepared to care for an embryo. This means it is all too easy for most women to become pregnant if they have sex. Whether they have an orgasm or not makes no difference to fertilization.

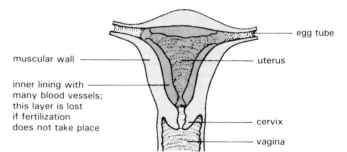

egg tube
muscular wall
uterus
inner lining with
many blood vessels;
this layer is lost
if fertilization
does not take place
cervix
vagina

If fertilization does not happen, the lining of the uterus breaks down and the blood-stained tissues pass out through the vagina. This is menstruation, and it takes a few days. It's also known as the menstrual period. Menstruation is only one part of the changes which take place during a month. Changes in the inner lining go like this:

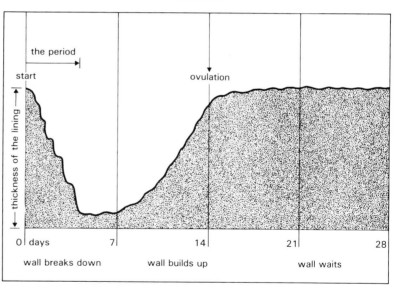

the period
start
ovulation
thickness of the lining

0 days    7    14    21    28

wall breaks down    wall builds up    wall waits

**OCTOBER 1982**

| Sunday | Monday | Tuesday | Wednesday | Thursday | Friday | Saturday |
|--------|--------|---------|-----------|----------|--------|----------|
|        |        |         |           |          | 1      | 2        |
| 3      | 4      | 5       | 6         | 7        | 8      | 9        |
| 10     | 11     | 12      | 13        | 14       | 15     | 16       |
| 17     | 18     | 19      | 20        | 21       | 22     | 23       |
| 24     | 25     | 26      | 27        | 28       | 29     | 30       |
| 31     |        |         |           |          |        |          |

Menstruation is controlled by four different hormones. They are made by the pituitary gland in the brain and the follicle cells in the ovary. Control is complicated, so it isn't surprising that when girls start to have periods they are often irregular. Women differ in the length and timing of their periods, and they may stop altogether in someone suffering great stress.

103

# Fertilization

Sperm must swim up the Fallopian tubes to fertilize the egg. The difficulties of the journey are great, even though, thanks to sexual intercourse, semen is shot out of the penis into the vagina near the cervix.

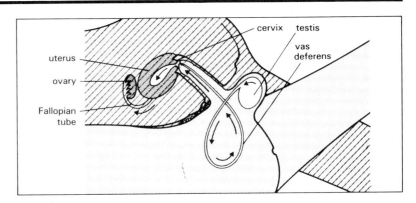

Perhaps one million sperm make it through the cervix into the uterus after an ejaculation. Only a few thousand arrive, thirty minutes later, at the entrance to a Fallopian tube. Even so, any egg in the tube becomes surrounded by a cloud of sperm – only one of which fertilizes the egg.

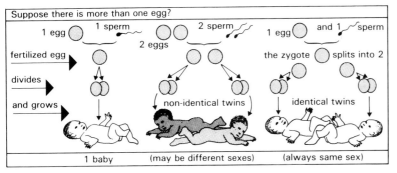

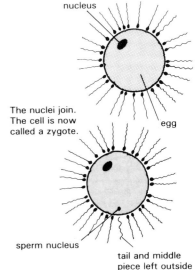

The nuclei join. The cell is now called a zygote.

The fertilized egg is moved by the beating of the cilia (small hairs) of the cells of the Fallopian tube. It drifts slowly down into the uterus and embeds itself in the uterus lining. The rest of the story is in Book 1.

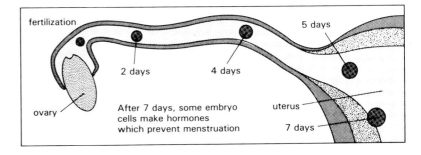

Details vary in animals other than humans. Some animals, such as cats, only ovulate after copulation (sexual intercourse). Many are only receptive at certain times of the year – when they are on heat. Copulation times vary a lot – gerbils take three seconds, other animals may spend hours locked together. But the aim is the same – fertilization.

104

# Summary and questions

## Summary

Male and female reproductive organs fit together in sexual intercourse in order to place sperm – male sex cells – well inside the female's body. Sperm are made in the testes and pass out of the male's body in a fluid – semen – through the penis during ejaculation. The penis fits into the female's vagina, so the sperm have only a small distance to swim to enter the uterus. They cross the uterus and travel along the Fallopian tubes towards the ovaries where eggs are stored. If there is an egg in the Fallopian tube, fertilization takes place. The fertilized egg travels to the uterus and embeds in the lining. If fertilization does not take place, the lining breaks down and is lost as part of the monthly menstrual cycle.

## Questions

1   Write this out, filling in the blanks.
    In animals, _____ gametes are sperm which must _____ towards the eggs. Sperm are made in the _____ which they leave by a tube called the _____ _____ which leads into the urethra, which goes down the middle of the _____. This organ fits neatly into the female's _____, provided enough preparation has been made. The internal organs of the female are the uterus and the _____, which contain the eggs. They are linked by the _____ tube and it is in this tube that _____ takes place. Sperm must swim through the _____ and across the _____ to reach the egg – from the sperm's point of view an enormous distance.

2.   Explain the difference between each of the following pairs:
     (a)  egg and sperm
     (b)  penis and clitoris
     (c)  vas deferens and urethra (in males)
     (d)  testes and ovary
     (e)  fertilization and sexual intercourse
     Give as much information as you can. Then describe the similarities between each pair.

3.   How would you explain to a young brother or sister the facts of life? Include in your explanation any pictures you might use.

4.   Explain how
     (a)  a penis becomes erect
     (b)  the uterus is prepared each month for a possible pregnancy
     (c)  twins – a boy and a girl – might happen
     (d)  the female's reproductive system prepares for intercourse

5.   Both testes and ovary are inside the body in an embryo. A boy's testes move into the scrotum just before birth. Look at the male reproductive system and suggest a way in which its layout supports the idea that testes change their position.

6.   (a)  Two fluids pass down the penis. What are they?
     (b)  How do the plumbing arrangements in the female differ from those in the male?

7.   You are given a hollowed-out pear, a cardboard tube, two plums and two straws. Make a model of the female reproductive organs.

8.   Make a list of names people use for the penis. Why do you think some people are upset when such words are printed in books?

# Making fertilization more likely

Darling!

Lunch!

Many female animals are unwilling to mate without a special pattern of behaviour – courtship – which overcomes other behaviour patterns.

This prevents a waste of energy and eggs. It is all geared to finding the best mate of the right species and sex at the right moment.

Male and female penguins look very much alike.

Ways of bringing the sexes together vary. Many animals use chemical signals.

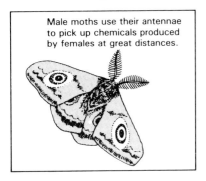

Male moths use their antennae to pick up chemicals produced by females at great distances.

Others use sound – like birds and frogs.

The male frog's throat amplifies croaks.

'I'm ready to mate' can be said with colours.

House sparrow males

in the breeding season

not ready to mate – yellow beak, duller colours

Courtship displays often sort out which males will father most of the next generation.

Seal bulls sorting out who is the strongest

Many animals go through courtship 'dances' – a 'step' by one animal triggers its partner to respond. Only suitable partners get it right, and one false step means no mating. In some cases these 'dances' keep the pair together. This can be important if rearing the young takes the efforts of two parents, and is commonest in animals like birds and mammals. Albatrosses have a 'dance' which leads to mating and makes them a long-term pair.

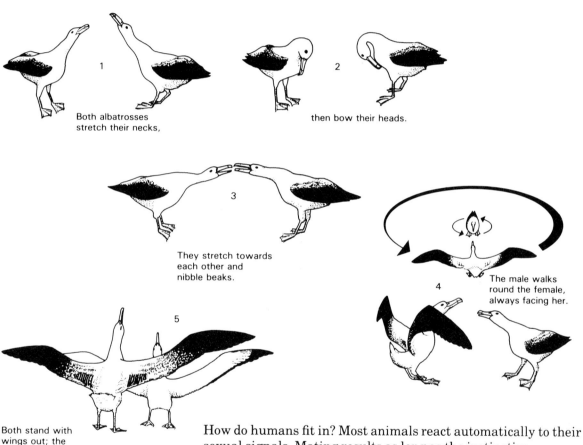

1 Both albatrosses stretch their necks,

2 then bow their heads.

3 They stretch towards each other and nibble beaks.

4 The male walks round the female, always facing her.

5 Both stand with wings out; the next step is mating.

How do humans fit in? Most animals react automatically to their sexual signals. Mating results as long as the instinctive programming of the two animals match. Human beings are animals, and they also have inherited sexual turn-ons. Sexual response is triggered and kept going in many ways – by exchanging eye signals, by stroking various parts of the body, and by smell (a natural smell is very important – stick to soap and water). Humans, unlike other animals, think about what they do, and sex is part of more than just getting an egg fertilized. For most people really satisfactory sex involves more than bare technique. It takes trust, time to explore each other, and lots of practice.

# Controlling fertilization

Given a fertility drug, a sheep may produce four lambs instead of one or two.

Understanding how fertilization happens means we can begin to control it. Hormones which control ovulation can be used to increase family size. Fertility drugs cause eggs to be released from the ovary. It is difficult to judge the dose which will release the right number of eggs.

Other sex hormones are used in the pill, which prevents eggs being released from the ovary – as long as it is taken regularly. The pill is one of several ways sperm can be prevented from reaching an egg (contraception).

A very safe couple

- stop egg release – the pill
- cut egg tube – sterilization
- prevent embedding of fertilized egg – IUD
- cover cervix – diaphragm
- kill sperm in the vagina – spermicide cream
- cover penis – sheath or condom
- cut vas deferens – sterilization

It is now possible to choose not to have children, or to choose when to have them and how many. The type of contraception should be chosen carefully. Some contraceptives can only be got from a doctor, and medical advice is useful anyway. For example – do all methods work equally well? The answer is no.

100

In one year, out of 100 sexually active women –

80 would get pregnant if they used no contraceptive

spermicide cream alone 30 babies

sheath or diaphragm and spermicide cream

rhythm method 35 babies result

sheath or diaphragm alone 20

on the pill, maybe 1 or 2

sterilized probably none

with IUDs 6

5

It looks as though sterilization is safest if you don't want children. In men it is particularly quick and easy. However, you should be sure you're not going to change your mind. Sterilization can sometimes be reversed, but not always.

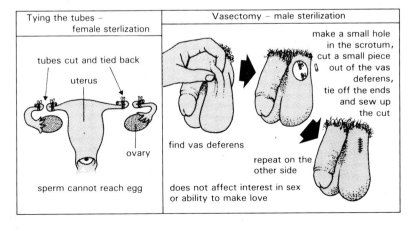

Tying the tubes – female sterilization

tubes cut and tied back

uterus

ovary

sperm cannot reach egg

Vasectomy – male sterilization

make a small hole in the scrotum, cut a small piece out of the vas deferens, tie off the ends and sew up the cut

find vas deferens

repeat on the other side

does not affect interest in sex or ability to make love

IUDs are useful because once they are in place they can be more or less forgotten. Some women cannot use them as they sometimes cause bleeding or cramps. IUDs work best in women who have had children.

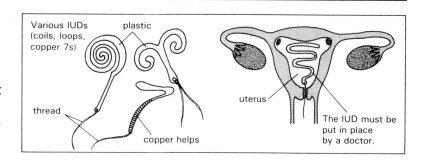

Barriers like sheaths and diaphragms are convenient for many people, but they are not very effective without a spermicide cream or foam placed inside the vagina to kill sperm. And even a small hole in the sheath or diaphragm makes it useless.

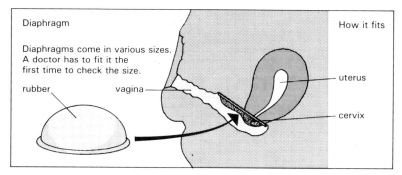

The egg is only in the tubes for a few days each month. The rhythm method relies on not making love during these days. For it to work, you must be able to find out which they are. Women who have regular cycles can work out when they ovulate by keeping a record of their body temperature. Not all women have regular cycles, and this makes the method risky. It is mostly used by people whose religion does not allow them to use other methods of contraception.

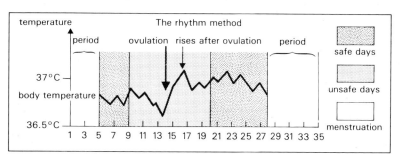

Each of these methods of contraception has advantages and problems. People use other ways to try to avoid pregnancy, but they work even less well. 'Just the once', doing it standing up or jumping up and down afterwards don't help a bit. It's very important to take proper precautions.

# VD

Venereal diseases (VD) are caused by organisms living in the reproductive system (and occasionally in the mouth or the end of the gut). Sexual activity gives the organisms a chance to travel. They enter a new host by openings like the mouth, the anus and the entrance to the reproductive organs. They range in size from crabs (pubic lice which can be seen) to microscopic organisms like Candida (a yeast which causes thrush – very itchy).

Two main types of VD are gonorrhoea (clap) and syphilis (pox) – both caused by microscopic organisms.

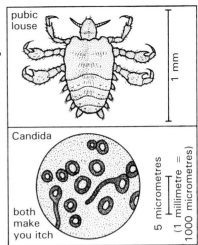

pubic louse

1 mm

Candida

both make you itch

5 micrometres

(1 millimetre = 1000 micrometres)

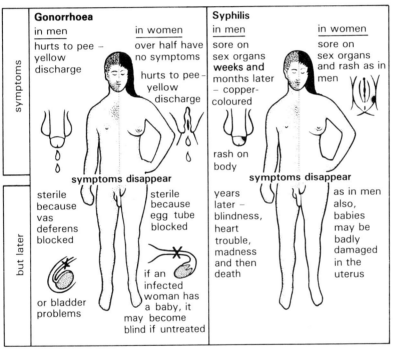

**symptoms**

**Gonorrhoea**

in men
hurts to pee – yellow discharge

in women
over half have no symptoms

hurts to pee – yellow discharge

**Syphilis**

in men
sore on sex organs **weeks and** months later – copper-coloured

rash on body

in women
sore on sex organs and rash as in men

**symptoms disappear**

**but later**

sterile because vas deferens blocked

or bladder problems

sterile because egg tube blocked

if an infected woman has a baby, it may become blind if untreated

**symptoms disappear**

years later – blindness, heart trouble, madness and then death

as in men also, babies may be badly damaged in the uterus

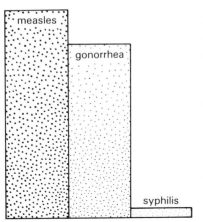

measles

gonorrhea

syphilis

Both diseases can be cured completely if treated early enough. They can unfortunately be caught again – and again. The graph gives a rough idea of how common they are compared to measles. There are probably many more cases of gonorrhoea as not everyone comes for treatment – which is free. It's a pity they don't, as gonorrhoea is increasing.

Many people are shy or embarrassed, especially about telling their lovers. Would you prefer to be told or not if there was a chance you had VD?

**LOVE IS**

Visiting the VD clinic together

# Summary and questions

## Summary

Animals signal that they are ready to mate in many ways, including scents and songs. Many show courtship patterns which help to get as many eggs as possible fertilized. People have some control over fertilization – fertility drugs increase the chances, contraceptives reduce them. Human sexuality has become more relaxed now that pregnancy is a matter of choice, but there are problems such as the increase in venereal disease.

## Questions

1. Imagine you are a book reviewer and you have been given this book to review. Write two pieces about the last fourteen pages (from 'Sexual reproduction in animals' to here).
   (a) Write one as though you did not approve of human sex being in a biology book: 'it should be about animals and plants, it's not a sexy magazine'.
   (b) Write the other as though you believed that textbooks should contain as much information about sex as this one does.

2. What is meant by the following? (Give examples.)
   (a) courtship
   (b) fertility drugs
   (c) contraception
   (d) venereal disease

3. What method of contraception would you advise for the following people?
   (a) a couple who have three children and think that's plenty
   (b) someone who hasn't a steady lover but who wants to be safe if an opportunity turns up
   (c) a woman who has one child and wants to wait a few years before having another
   (d) a young couple not ready to start a family
   Give a reason for your suggestion in each case.

4. Explain how the following animals find a mate:   (a) moths,   (b) albatrosses,   (c) sparrows,   (d) frogs,   (e) a dog or a cat.

5. (a) The organisms which cause gonorrhoea and syphilis die as soon as they are not protected by the warmth and dampness of the body. Knowing this, do you think it is possible to catch VD from a lavatory seat?
   (b) Far more people catch gonorrhoea than syphilis in England, although both are easy to treat. Why do you think there is less syphilis around?
   (c) During the last day or so, David has noticed that he has leaked a little yellowish goo and that his privates itch. It doesn't quite fit with the symptoms for gonorrhoea in this book but he is a bit worried – especially as he's been to a party lately where he could have picked up a dose. What should he do, and why? Would you? Why?

6. An abortion occurs when a child is born before it is able to survive outside the womb. When this happens naturally it is called a miscarriage. It may happen for various reasons – for example, if the mother has an accident or the foetus is very abnormal. People sometimes choose to have an abortion, perhaps if the pregnancy is unwanted, or tests show that the baby is going to be abnormal. Do you think people should be able to have abortions whenever they want to? Give your reasons.
   (Don't write anything until you have tried to find out more information about abortion, and discussed the problem with other people. Boys should ask girls how they feel about the subject.)

# Gametes, chromosomes and sex

In many ways the members of a family are alike – they have the same number and kinds of legs, ears, lungs and toes. There are often family likenesses in small details. If plants and animals always budded asexually off their parents like strawberry plants, the members of a family line would be exactly the same. This doesn't happen. Hair colour or allergies may be different. A list of family differences may be quite long. How does sexual reproduction produce all the differences and all the similarities?

'He's got his father's nose all right!'

We know that the nucleus is important – only the nucleus of a sperm (or pollen grain) enters the egg at fertilization.

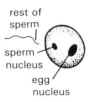

rest of sperm

sperm nucleus

egg nucleus

Inside a dividing cell, rod-like chromosomes can be seen. The chromosomes carry all the instructions for the growth of a new organism.

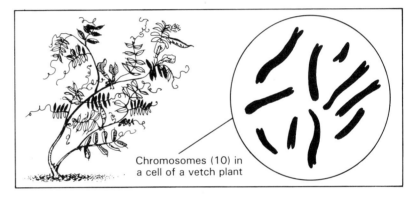

Chromosomes (10) in a cell of a vetch plant

Whatever the number (different in different species) a gamete has half as many chromosomes as an ordinary body cell.

| | Number of chromosomes in | | |
| --- | --- | --- | --- |
| | egg cells | sperm or pollen cells | body cells |
| Hawkweed | 4 | 4 | 8 |
| Sedge | 21 | 21 | 42 |
| Hen | 18 | 18 | 36 |
| Man | 23 | 23 | 46 |
| Kangaroo | 6 | 6 | 12 |

The chromosomes in a body cell can be sorted out into pairs – which fits with the idea that half came from one parent, half from the other. Each body cell has two complete sets of chromosomes, one set from each parent.

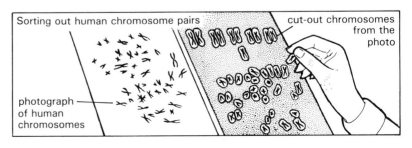

Sorting out human chromosome pairs

cut-out chromosomes from the photo

photograph of human chromosomes

Each chromosome contains the instructions for many different characteristics. For example, in human beings, everything that goes to make males and females different is controlled by just one of the twenty-three pairs of chromosomes. It is the same in many other animals.

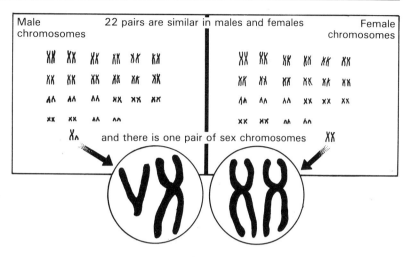

Males are said to be XY and females XX – mostly because of the shapes of the sex chromosomes.

People still cannot choose the sex of their children, but we do know how sex is inherited.

**From the mother (XX).** The egg contains twenty-two 'body' chromosomes and one sex chromosome. It can only be an X chromosome. So all eggs have an X.

**From the father (XY).** Sperm also have twenty-two body chromosomes. Half the sperm have an X sex chromosome. The rest have a Y chromosome.

If one of the ⟨x⟩ sperms reaches the egg first and fertilizes it, the result is ⟨xx⟩ a girl.

But there are just as many ⟨y⟩ sperms, and if one of them arrives first the result is [xy] a boy.

In small families there may be more boys than girls just by chance. In the whole population, equal numbers of boys and girls might be expected. In fact slightly more boys than girls are born, though we are not sure why.

Boy babies are more delicate and more of them die than girl babies, so the numbers balance by the end of childhood.

Very rarely, mistakes happen and a sperm or egg either has an extra sex chromosome or no sex chromosome. People born with the wrong number of sex chromosomes are usually sterile – they cannot have children themselves.

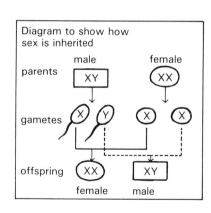

Diagram to show how sex is inherited

# Gamete formation-meiosis

Sex cells are not the result of mitosis like ordinary body cells (Book 1). After mitosis the daughter cells have the same chromosomes as the parent cells.

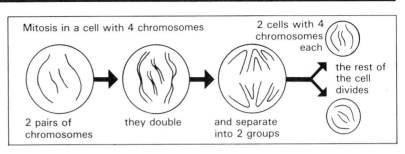

Mitosis in a cell with 4 chromosomes

2 cells with 4 chromosomes each

the rest of the cell divides

2 pairs of chromosomes — they double — and separate into 2 groups

After **meiosis** or **reduction division**, which only happens in the sex organs, each daughter cell has half the chromosomes of the parent cell. The daughter cells may be male or female gametes, depending on whether they are in an ovary or testis (or stamen).

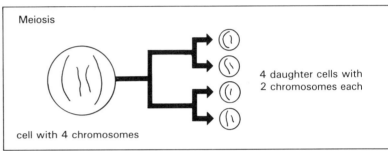

Meiosis

4 daughter cells with 2 chromosomes each

cell with 4 chromosomes

Each of the daughter cells has one of each type of chromosome. Fertilization produces a cell with two full sets of chromosomes.

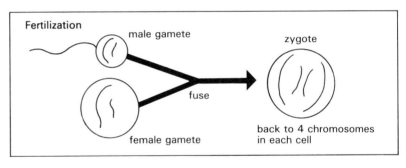

Fertilization

male gamete

zygote

fuse

female gamete

back to 4 chromosomes in each cell

One interesting result of meiosis is that all the gametes produced are different. Before looking at meiosis in more detail in order to explain how this happens, you need to know a little more about chromosomes.

## Chromosomes and genes

We have only twenty-three pairs of chromosomes to carry the instructions for the whole human body. Each chromosome carries the information for many chemical reactions. For example, we believe that the instructions for making both salivary amylase (it's in Book 1) and the Rhesus blood antigens are part of the same chromosome. The instructions for a particular trait or characteristic are called a **gene**. There are genes for eye colour, blood type and so on.

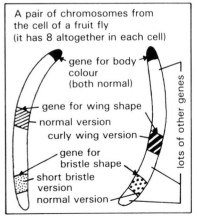

A pair of chromosomes from the cell of a fruit fly (it has 8 altogether in each cell)

gene for body colour (both normal)

gene for wing shape
normal version
curly wing version

gene for bristle shape
short bristle version
normal version

lots of other genes

You have two copies of each gene, one in each of a pair of chromosomes. They may be identical or they may have slightly different effects. For example, you have two genes for eye colour, but one might be for blue and one for brown eyes. (More later.)

One copy of each gene came from your father, the other from your mother.

## Meiosis in more detail

For each cell that divides, meiosis results in four gametes. The chromosomes double, and then divide first into two groups and then again so there are four groups.

In the diagrams, the dark-coloured chromosomes are from the father's side.

1. It's another 4-chromosome cell.

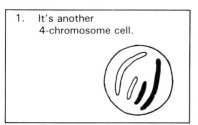

2. The chromosomes double.

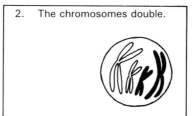

3. Pairs of chromosomes lie alongside each other.

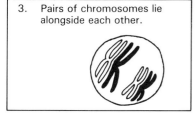

4. They twist around each other and exchange bits of chromosome material (and so exchange genes).

5. They move to the middle of the cell.

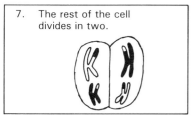

6. Pairs of chromosomes separate – this is the first division.

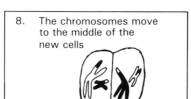

7. The rest of the cell divides in two.

8. The chromosomes move to the middle of the new cells

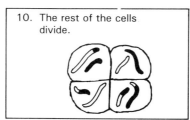

9. The chromosome copies separate – this is the second division.

10. The rest of the cells divide.

The sex cells are a mixture of the chromosome material of both parents.

As humans have forty-six chromosomes, not four, in their normal body cells, it is not surprising that one set of parents can produce very different children. However, each one has all the information to grow into an adult human.

# What are chromosomes made of?

The short answer to this question is 'protein and DNA'. A longer answer might be:
**Proteins** – which may help to give the chromosome its structure (by providing a framework for the DNA) and help regulate the action of DNA; and **DNA** (deoxyribose nucleic acid). DNA is a molecule which acts as a plan for the cell. In a similar way, a recipe is a plan for a cake but not the cake itself.

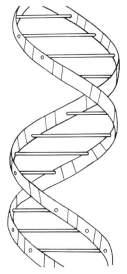

DNA is a long molecule made of 2 twisted strands.

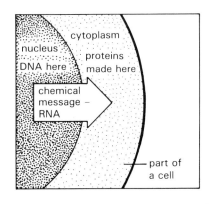

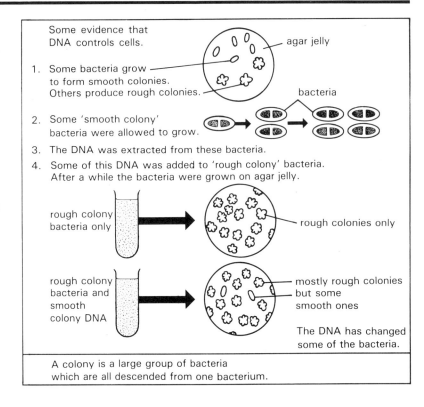

Some evidence that DNA controls cells.

1. Some bacteria grow to form smooth colonies. Others produce rough colonies.

2. Some 'smooth colony' bacteria were allowed to grow.

3. The DNA was extracted from these bacteria.

4. Some of this DNA was added to 'rough colony' bacteria. After a while the bacteria were grown on agar jelly.

rough colony bacteria only → rough colonies only

rough colony bacteria and smooth colony DNA → mostly rough colonies but some smooth ones

The DNA has changed some of the bacteria.

A colony is a large group of bacteria which are all descended from one bacterium.

DNA is a very long thin molecule.

It does two essential things supremely well.
1. It can copy itself accurately. This is important every time a cell divides.
2. It can be translated into protein form by the cell. The proteins can be enzymes, or ones which are important to the structure of a cell. The proteins a cell makes decide what kind of cell it is. All the cells together decide the characteristics of an organism.

The length of DNA which codes for a protein (or part of a protein) is the section of a chromosome we call a gene.

**Genetic engineering** involves using biological tricks to snip out of a cell's DNA a section which codes for a protein we need. This DNA is put in another cell (at the moment this is usually a bacterium) which is allowed to multiply and make the protein we want. As this book was being written, there was a lot of interest in making insulin (a hormone needed by diabetics) and interferon (the body's chemical defence against viruses). By the time you read this page, I am sure much more will be possible.

# Summary and questions

## Summary

Chromosomes are rod-like bodies in the nucleus of each cell which carry the instructions for making new cells. They are made of protein and DNA. During meiosis, the number of chromosomes in a cell is halved. As the result of meiosis, gametes are produced. A gene is a section of DNA which codes for a protein and so for a characteristic of the organism. In gametes, genes have been shuffled, which means that the offspring in a family differ from each other and from their parents.

## Questions

1. Do you think it would be a good idea if people were allowed to choose the sex of their babies? Give your reasons.

2. Fill in the numbers and write out the passage below.
   Human body cells have _____ chromosomes. Of these, _____ are sex chromosomes. Organisms have different numbers of chromosomes. For example, a kangaroo has _____ chromosomes in each body cell. Gametes always have _____ the number of chromosomes found in a body cell.

3. Explain the connection between
   (a) a chromosome and a gene
   (b) meiosis and gametes
   (c) sex and sex chromosomes

4. Explain why
   (a) organisms which reproduce asexually have the same chromosomes as their parent
   (b) you would expect equal numbers of boys and girls to be born (though in fact more boys are born than girls)

5. Here is a description of mitosis. Rewrite it for meiosis, replacing the underlined phrases if necessary and adding anything you think is important.
   Mitosis is the type of cell division which produces ordinary body cells. It can happen in many places in an organism. The daughter cells are identical with each other and with the parent cell. First the chromosomes double. Then the copies separate into groups at opposite ends of the cell. The cytoplasm of the cell divides to form two daughter cells. These can then divide again or become active body cells such as muscle cells.

6. Think of a family you know (mother, father, two or more children). Make a list of similarities between the children which you think might be inherited. Make a list of differences between the children. How can you explain the differences?

7. A cell undergoes meiosis. If it is in a testis, four sperm cells result. If it is in an ovary, only one of the four cells produced becomes a mature egg cell. Why do you think this is? (Hint: size.)

# Genetics 1

We can't see genes but we can see their effects. Studying the visible patterns of inheritance and trying to explain them is called **genetics**. The patterns were first explored using organisms like Drosophila (the fruit fly), mice or corn – not human beings. Why?

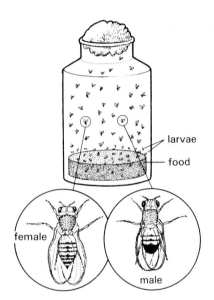

| Drosophila (and smaller organisms) | Humans (and large animals) |
| --- | --- |
| You can control which fruit fly mates with which. | People do **not** like having mates chosen for them in order to do an experiment. |
| Fruit flies breed when 14 days old – you can look at many generations in a short time. | It takes years before the next generation is produced. |
| Fruit flies have hundreds of offspring. This means the results you get are less likely to be just chance. | Families are small. |
| Sharp differences in appearance are easy to study genetically. | Shades of colour, height and so on are difficult to study. |
| Lots of fruit flies can live in a small space. They're easy to handle. | Take up a lot of room. |

From organisms like Drosophila we have learnt to understand inheritance. There have been many experiments – here is one of them.

Start with pure-bred flies. A pure-bred organism comes from a long line of individuals which have bred true for a characteristic. For example, if we mate two pure-bred short-winged flies then all their offspring will have short wings.

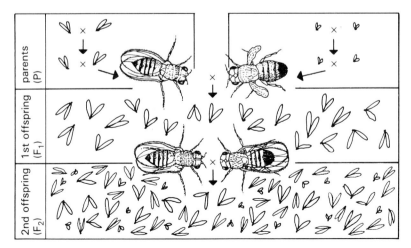

A pure-bred long-winged fly mates with a pure-bred short-winged fly.

All the hundreds of offspring have long wings.

Two of these are mated. For every three of their offspring with long wings, there is one with short wings.

How can this be explained – what happened to 'short wings' in the middle?

**The explanation** goes like this. We know that offspring inherit half their genes from each parent. Suppose there is a gene for wing length and it comes in two versions: **N** is the version for normal wing length and **n** is the version for short wings. Each gamete is Ⓝ or ⓝ and each adult has two copies of the gene – one from each parent.
We can explain what we see like this:

Parents are **NN** and **nn**.
Their gametes are Ⓝ and ⓝ.
and the first offspring (F₁) must be **Nn**.
The effect of **n** is hidden by **N**.
But what happens if we do some breeding?
Each of the F₁ parents is **Nn**.
They each have Ⓝ and ⓝ gametes.

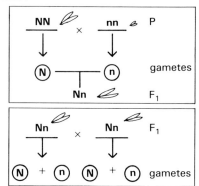

There are four possible combinations by chance:

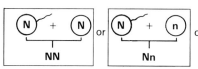

So F₂ (second offspring) are three long-winged flies to every one short-winged fly.
This 3 : 1 ratio is a sign that both parents have a mixture of genes.

Genetics has some useful words – handy for keeping explanations and questions short.

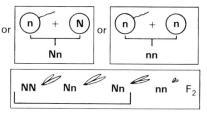

or use a Punnet square to work it out:

| sperm \ eggs | N | n |
|---|---|---|
| N | NN | Nn |
| n | Nn | nn |

| Word | Meaning | Fruit fly examples |
|---|---|---|
| **Homozygous** | The two versions of a gene are the same. | **NN** and **nn** flies were homozygous for wing length |
| **Heterozygous** | The two versions of a gene are different. | **Nn** were heterozygous flies. |
| **Recessive** | A gene which can be hidden by another. Its effects are only seen in a homozygote. | **n** is a recessive gene. |
| **Dominant** | A gene which hides another. Its effects are seen in both homozygotes and heterozygotes. | **N** is a dominant gene. |

On the next two pages these ideas are used to explain some other situations.

# Genetics 2

More genetics examples – useful if you get stuck on the problems.

1    Coleus plants can have deep-lobed leaves or shallow-lobed leaves.

If a cross is set up between **homozygous** shallow-lobed and deep-lobed plants then the offspring is deep-lobed – so the deep-lobed gene (**L**) is dominant over the shallow-lobed gene (**l**).

Here is the cross:

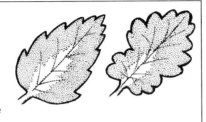

The offspring are **heterozygous**.

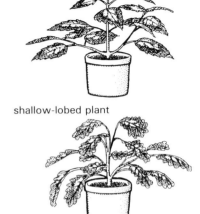

shallow-lobed plant

deep-lobed plant

## Genotype and phenotype

**genotype** – the genes an organism has

**phenotype** – what it looks like (the effect of its genes)

**LL** and **Ll** plants have the same phenotype but different genotypes.

Another way of working out Mary's children:

|  | eggs | | |
|---|---|---|---|
| **sperm** | | **C** | **c** |
| **C** | | | |
| **c** | | | |

With all the possible combinations filled in:

|  | eggs | | |
|---|---|---|---|
| **sperm** | | **C** | **c** |
| **C** | | CC | Cc |
| **c** | | Cc | cc |

2    A normal man marries an albino woman. (Albino means having no colour in the skin. White mice with pink eyes are albino.) The gene for albino (**c**) is recessive compared to the gene for normal colour (**C**).

Kids (F₁) must be normal-coloured as they have one dominant gene for colour.

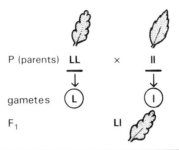

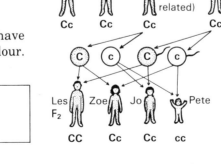

**key**
people **CC**, **Cc** or **cc**
gametes **C** or **c**

Mary can have an albino child is she marries a man who also carries an albino gene. This is not very likely, as the albino gene is not common. If she does, there is still only one chance in four that a child will be albino.

## 3 A family tree – and explaining it

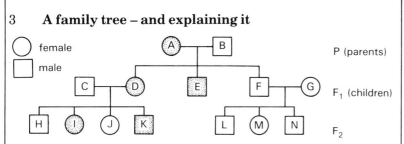

female (circle)
male (square)

P (parents)
F₁ (children)
F₂

All the shaded people (like A) have six fingers. The others have five. The things to note are: six-fingered people (A) can have five-fingered children (F); and as long as one parent has six fingers (D), some of the kids have six fingers (I and K). So a good guess is that the six-finger gene **F** is dominant over the five-finger gene **f**. Capital letters are used for dominant genes. A is probably heterozygous. Fill in the family tree and see if it works.

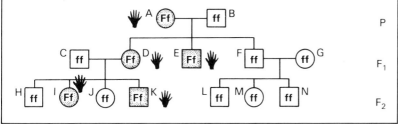

P
F₁
F₂

Normal feathers hold together.
Frizzle feathers do not.
These are very frizzled.

Not all genes work as simply as the ones we've looked at. Sometimes neither version of a gene is dominant – the heterozygote looks like a mixture. This is called **incomplete dominance**. Here's an example.

**Monohybrid** crosses (all the ones we've discussed so far) involve only one set of genes. Things get very complicated when more genes are involved in one characteristic.

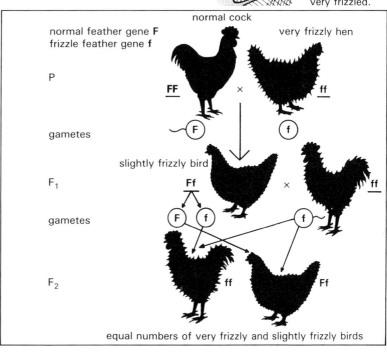

normal feather gene **F**
frizzle feather gene **f**

normal cock
very frizzly hen

P
FF × ff

gametes
F f

F₁
slightly frizzly bird
Ff × ff

gametes
F f f

F₂
ff Ff

equal numbers of very frizzly and slightly frizzly birds

121

# What Mendel did

Mendel was an Austrian monk who worked over 100 years ago. He discovered the basic laws of inheritance. In his monastery he did many experiments with garden peas. The choice of plant was fortunate – garden peas normally self-pollinate and usually breed true (that is, they are homozygous) and they have clear-cut characteristics. Mendel carefully cross-pollinated his true-breeding peas. The table shows some of his results.

| P (pure-bred) | F₁ (hybrids) | F₂ |
|---|---|---|
| round × wrinkled | all round | 5474 round + 1850 wrinkles or about 3 : 1 |
| green pods × yellow pods | all green | 428 green + 152 yellow or about 3 : 1 |
| tall × short | all tall | 787 tall + 277 short or about 3 : 1 |

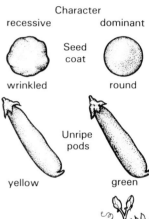

Character

| recessive | | dominant |
|---|---|---|
| wrinkled | Seed coat | round |
| yellow | Unripe pods | green |

Mendel did not know about genes, but he worked out that his results could be explained by an organism inheriting 'factors' (genes) from its parents.

He used the idea of dominant and recessive factors to explain the way some characteristics – like wrinkled seeds – disappeared in the F₁ mixtures or **hybrids**.

Here, for example, is the explanation for the cross between round and wrinkled seeds.

(**R** – gene for round coat)
(**r** – gene for wrinkled coat)

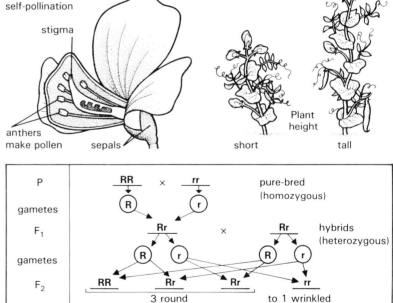

enclosed flower means self-pollination
stigma
anthers make pollen
sepals

Plant height
short        tall

| P | RR × rr | | pure-bred (homozygous) |
| gametes | R    r | | |
| F₁ | Rr × Rr | | hybrids (heterozygous) |
| gametes | R  r    R  r | | |
| F₂ | RR  Rr  Rr  rr | | |
|  | 3 round | to 1 wrinkled | |

Mendel sent his results to a Swiss botanist who did not think they were important. No one realised how important his ideas were until other people investigating the same ideas using fruit flies. Mendel was dead by then.

# Summary and questions

## Summary

For any characteristic an organism has at least two genes – one from each parent. They may be the same (homozygous) or different (heterozygous). Versions of a gene which always show their effects are dominant. Versions of a gene which can be hidden are called recessive. Genotype refers to the genes an organism has, phenotype to the way it looks. The original work was done by Mendel using garden peas. Like other useful organisms for studying genetics, peas reproduce quickly, are no trouble and have clear-cut alternative characteristics. The best way to get on top of genetics is to do lots of problems.

## Questions

1. Explain the difference between the following pairs:
   (a) fruit flies and elephants as suitable organisms for genetic studies
   (b) hybrid and pure-bred organisms
   (c) homozygous and heterozygous organisms
   (d) recessive and dominant versions of a gene
   (e) the way coleus leaf edges are inherited and the way frizzle hen feathers are inherited
   (f) genotype and phenotype (use examples)

2. Look back to 'Genetics 2', example 2 – the family with an albino mother.
   (a) Name all the homozygous people in this family.
   (b) Name all the heterozygous people in this family. Which people have the same genotype as Dave?
   (c) What genes must a person have to be albino?
   Look at example 3 – the family where some people have six fingers.
   (d) Which is recessive – the six-finger version of the gene or the five-finger version?
   (e) Give the letters of two people who are heterozygous for this gene. Give the letter of a person with the same genotype as B.
   (f) How many children does F have? How many are boys?

   (g) How many grandchildren does A have? How many are girls? Where did E inherit the **f** gene from? and the **F** gene?
   Look at example 4 – the chicken feathers.
   (h) What genes does a slightly frizzly bird have? Is the frizzle or the non-frizzle feather gene dominant?
   (i) What do you get if you cross a slightly frizzly bird with a very frizzly bird?
   (j) What do you get if you cross a slightly frizzly bird with a normal bird?

3. (a) A pure-breeding black bull is crossed with a pure-breeding red cow. Their offspring are all black. Choose letters to represent the genes and draw a diagram which explains this cross. Which version of the colour gene is recessive? Which animals are heterozygous for this gene?
   (b) Two curly-winged Drosophila are mated. Their offspring are 341 curly-winged and 110 normal-winged flies. How could you explain this?

4. (a) In cattle, a horned animal crossed with a hornless animal sometimes produces only hornless cattle. Is horned or hornless the dominant gene? Choose letters for the horned and hornless versions of the gene and write out the cross. Which animals are heterozygous?
   (b) Sometimes, though, a horned animal crossed with a hornless animal produces equal numbers of horned and hornless animals. Can you explain what has happened?

# Mutations-genetic change

Mutations are changes in genetic material. Sometimes large parts of a chromosome are affected, sometimes the change is within one gene.

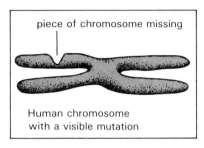

piece of chromosome missing

Human chromosome with a visible mutation

Nearly all mutations are harmful. This is hardly surprising, as the existing genes of an organism already work well together. Missing genes, extra genes and changed genes are almost bound to upset the system. It can mean death. Not all mutations cause changes as large as the ones in the example.

A few mutations are useful to the organisms in which they happen. Our distant ancestors did not look like us, judging by their fossilized bones. As useful mutations happened, organisms gradually became more like those living today.

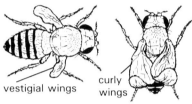

vestigial wings

curly wings

These fruit flies have mutations which would mean their death in the wild.

Mistakes in genes can happen anyway, but more mutations happen when an organism is exposed to radiation or chemicals like mustard gas and LSD. Mutation in body cells may result in a cancer. Mutations in cells which become gametes mean that the mistakes can be passed to offspring – genetic diseases may result. This is very worrying as humans are using more sources of radiation (nuclear bombs, nuclear power stations) and more new chemicals which can get into our food or the air we breathe. It is for this reason that pregnant women should be X-rayed as rarely as possible.

## Genetic diseases

An example – sickle-cell anaemia.
A person with sickle-cell anaemia has red blood cells which become drawn out and cannot carry oxygen properly round the body. It is caused by a mistake in a gene involved in making haemoglobin – usually called $Hb^S$. The normal gene is $Hb^N$.

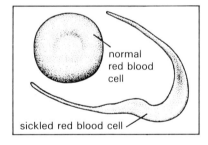

normal red blood cell

sickled red blood cell

Here is a family in which the parents are both heterozygous for this gene. Dominance is incomplete.

There are many genetic diseases, such as cystic fibrosis, phenylketanuria and Huntington's chorea. Most are unpleasant, and if their names are unfamiliar it is because mostly they are rare.

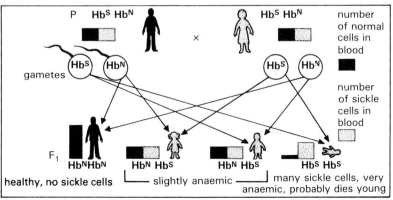

P $Hb^S Hb^N$ × $Hb^S Hb^N$

number of normal cells in blood

gametes $Hb^S$ $Hb^N$ $Hb^S$ $Hb^N$

number of sickle cells in blood

$F_1$ $Hb^N Hb^N$ $Hb^N Hb^S$ $Hb^N Hb^S$ $Hb^S Hb^S$

healthy, no sickle cells — slightly anaemic — many sickle cells, very anaemic, probably dies young

One special group of mutations are the **sex-linked** ones where changes happen in the X chromosome. The result is interesting. If a man has the mutated gene as part of the X chromosome the effects will show, as the Y chromosome hasn't got a gene to make up for the deficiency. If a woman has one X chromosome with a mutation, and one normal one, she appears to be normal – but she is a **carrier**. A woman only shows the effects if she has two damaged X chromosomes.

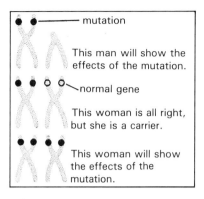

— mutation

This man will show the effects of the mutation.

normal gene

This woman is all right, but she is a carrier.

This woman will show the effects of the mutation.

**Colour-blindness** is a fairly common example. Sex chromosomes have genes for characteristics besides sex. The ability to see colour is one of them. Here is a family in which the mother has a hidden gene for colour-blindness. Her sight is normal.

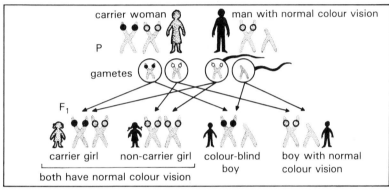

carrier woman  man with normal colour vision

P

gametes

F₁

carrier girl  non-carrier girl  colour-blind boy  boy with normal colour vision

both have normal colour vision

The clues to sex linkage are:
(a) It is nearly always males who suffer.
(b) They only suffer from sex-linked diseases because their mothers are carriers. From their fathers they inherit a Y chromosome which isn't affected.
(c) You can only tell that a woman is a carrier if she has sons who are affected.

A famous sex-linked disease is haemophilia. Haemophiliacs – 'bleeders' – have blood which doesn't clot properly. They often die young. It is a rare disease, but Queen Victoria was a carrier for it, perhaps as the result of a mutation in a gene in one of the X chromosomes she inherited from her parents. She passed it on to her children, and the gene spread through several European royal houses. It no doubt affected history.

Queen Victoria surrounded by some of her family

Two of her daughters were carriers of haemophilia. One married the Tsar of Russia.

# Using genetics-people

There is always a small risk of having a handicapped child, but no one would deliberately have one.

Genetic counselling helps couples to decide how great the risk is for them. Perhaps someone comes from a family in which haemophilia is known.

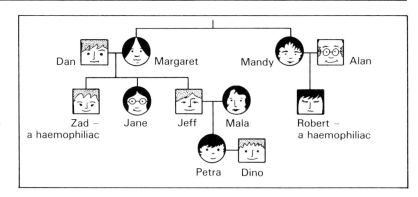

Petra is worried – is she a carrier for haemophilia? Should she risk having children? In fact she is clear – her X chromosomes must both be normal. If Jeff had inherited a damaged X chromosome from Margaret, as Zad did, he'd be a haemophiliac himself. Petra can have children, and they'll be normal.

What about Jane? She could have inherited her mother's normal X chromosome, but equally she could have the damaged one. She can't tell without having children. If she is a carrier, half her sons are likely to be haemophiliac. Would you risk it?

Jane may soon have another choice, although for haemophilia the test is still being tried out. Cells from the fluid around an embryo can be sampled and checked for chromosome damage.

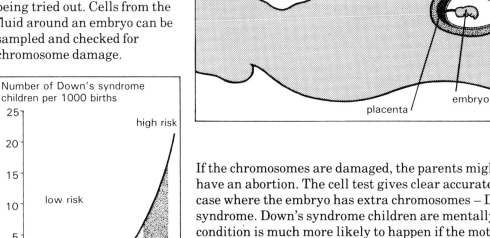

**Number of Down's syndrome children per 1000 births**

```
25
         high risk
20

15
   low risk
10

5

    20  25  30  35  40  45
age of mother at time of birth,
in years
```

If the chromosomes are damaged, the parents might choose to have an abortion. The cell test gives clear accurate results in a case where the embryo has extra chromosomes – Down's syndrome. Down's syndrome children are mentally retarded. This condition is much more likely to happen if the mother is over 40.

Knowing the risk, an older woman might choose not to have a child, or to have a cell test and perhaps an abortion. Only the parents can make decisions like this, but it helps if they can be given clear advice about risks.

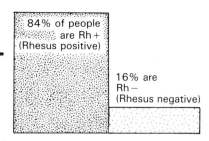

84% of people are Rh+ (Rhesus positive)

16% are Rh− (Rhesus negative)

Even without genetic diseases in the family, genetics helps to avoid problems. Humans have many kinds of blood groups. The **Rhesus** group is important in pregnancy. Most people have Rh+ blood.

Occasionally a Rh− woman marries an Rh+ man. Half the children inherit Rh+ blood from him. If Rh+ blood cells from an embryo leak into the mothers blood, her body defence system is sensitized against Rh+ blood. The first Rh+ baby is all right, but the blood cells of the next Rh+ baby may be clumped together by the mother's blood system. A simple blood test can warn a couple of the danger. The mother can have treatment after each birth to prevent her system becoming sensitized.

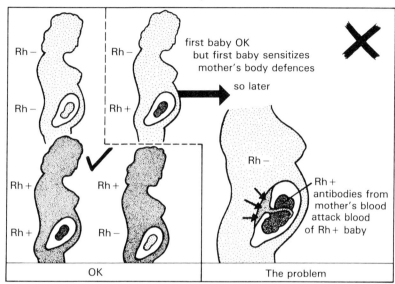

Rh− Rh−

Rh− Rh+

first baby OK but first baby sensitizes mother's body defences so later

Rh+ Rh+

Rh+ Rh−

Rh−

Rh+ antibodies from mother's blood attack blood of Rh+ baby

OK

The problem

### Genetics and legal tangles

The genetics of blood groups can help to sort out babies which are mixed up in hospital, or help to find the father. It works like this. The ABO blood system is important when transfusing blood. It is the result of one gene which is found in three different versions – **A**, **B**, or **i**.

| Blood group | Genotype |
| --- | --- |
| A | AA or Ai |
| B | BB or Bi |
| AB | AB |
| O | ii |

Ed suspects Marta has not been faithful. In particular he thinks weedy Mark is not his – unlike his favourite son Pete who is much more like himself. He insists on blood tests. Here are the results.

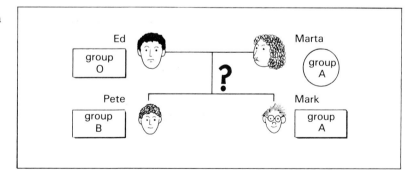

Ed — group O

Marta — group A

Pete — group B

Mark — group A

Oops – a pity he did that really. Ed has to be **ii**. Mark could easily be his son with an **A** gene from Marta and an **i** gene from Ed. But Pete! – he could have an **i** from Marta but never a **B** from Ed – Mark might well be Ed's but not Pete. What will Ed do? Write the next step in this drama yourself.

# Using genetics-artificial selection

We do not breed people to order, but over the years we have made big changes in the animals and plants that are important to us. We have done it by selective breeding. Picking out the most promising varieties, we breed them rather than eat them.

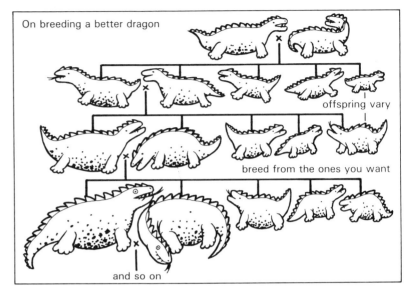

On breeding a better dragon

offspring vary

breed from the ones you want

and so on

This is the way from wild pigs to pork pigs,

from grasses to wheat,

and many more.

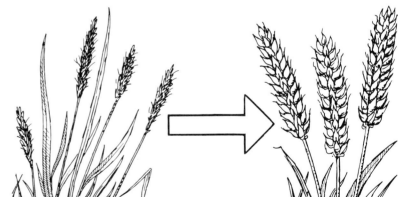

It can take many generations. Sometimes big advances have been made as the result of a rare useful mutation. Work continues – more productive rice, disease-resistant plants and faster-growing cattle may all help to provide the growing human population of the world with food.

# Summary and questions

## Summary
Completely new genetic material is the result of mutations or changes, such as loss of parts of chromosomes or changes in small pieces of DNA. A few changes are useful to the organism, but most mutations are harmful and in humans they may cause genetic diseases. Understanding the laws of genetics helps predict and so avoid genetic diseases. It can also sort out some legal problems. People have used genetic ideas for a long time (even if they didn't know it) to breed better plants and animals.

## Questions

1. Explain what is meant by the following (with examples)
   (a) mutation
   (b) genetic disease
   (c) sex-linked genes
   (d) genetic counselling
   (e) artificial selection
   (f) a carrier (as in colour-blindness)

2. Explain why
   (a) a Rhesus positive (Rh+) woman does not have to worry about the blood group of the man she marries
   (b) people with sickle-cell anaemia get tired easily
   (c) in the haemophiliac family, it is reasonable to believe that Margaret inherited the damaged X chromosome from her mother, rather than that it happened as a mutation in her own ovaries.

3. The study of genetics is very important to humans, but it is often hard to understand human genetic patterns. Why? (Look back to the last section for hints.)

4. A farmer would like his cattle to be hornless. Most of his herd are hornless but every so often a few horned ones are born. He guesses that the gene for horns is recessive to the gene for no horns, and that some of his hornless animals are heterozygous. What breeding plan could he follow to try and get a true-breeding (homozygous) hornless herd?

5. Huntington's chorea is a very rare and fatal disease of the nervous system. It does not develop until middle age. A man in his twenties learns that his father has Huntington's chorea. It is caused by a dominant gene (**not** carried on a sex chromosome).
   (a) What are the chances that he, the son, will also have it?
   (b) If the son does not develop the disease, what are the chances that his children will have Huntington's chorea?
   To work this out, choose a letter for the Huntington's chorea gene and for its normal version. Draw the family tree, then fill in the genotypes as far as you can.

6. A man who has slight sickle-cell anaemia marries a normal woman.
   (a) Can they produce normal children?
   (b) Can they have children with severe sickle-cell anaemia?
   (c) If they have four children, how many are likely to show some signs of sickle-cell anaemia? Explain your answers.

7. Two babies were born in hospital on a night when there was a blackout. It was possible that their identity bracelets got mixed up, so blood tests were done. Here are the results:

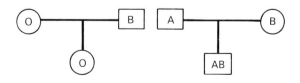

Are the babies with the right parents? Explain your answer.

# Evolution-the theory

It has long been known that life on earth has changed as time has passed.

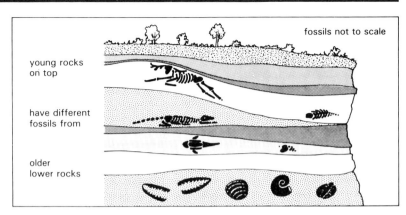

young rocks on top

have different fossils from

older lower rocks

fossils not to scale

There have been many ideas about how this happened, but the theory that most biologists accept today is based on that of Charles Darwin.

Darwin in 1854

As a young man, Darwin travelled around the world in HMS Beagle as ship's naturalist. He was puzzled by many of the things he saw. For example, the Galapagos Islands each have their own species of giant tortoise. The animals are clearly related but slightly different. The same was true of the finches on the islands. How could this be?

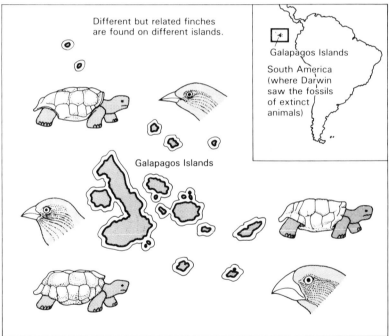

Different but related finches are found on different islands.

Galapagos Islands

South America (where Darwin saw the fossils of extinct animals)

Galapagos Islands

Darwin's answer was **natural selection**. We now know more about genetics than Darwin, and as a result today's version of his theory is a little different from his own version. It looks as though this is what happens:

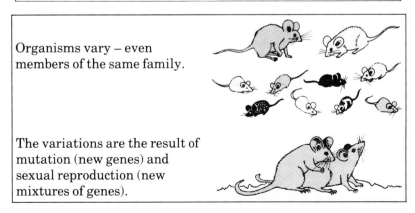

Organisms vary – even members of the same family.

The variations are the result of mutation (new genes) and sexual reproduction (new mixtures of genes).

Many more organisms are produced than grow up and reproduce. Most of them die.

Some variations are adaptive – they help an animal to survive and reproduce.

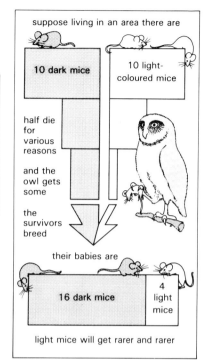

suppose living in an area there are

10 dark mice

10 light-coloured mice

half die for various reasons

and the owl gets some

the survivors breed

their babies are

16 dark mice

4 light mice

light mice will get rarer and rarer

Organisms with the best adaptations survive and have offspring, which inherit the adaptations. These useful characteristics become more common in a group of organisms. The group changes as it adapts to its environment, because the less well-adapted die, or do not produce as many offspring as the others. This is natural selection.

Once a group is adapted to its environment, natural selection means it does not change much, unless the environment changes.

These odd piles are produced by mats of blue-green algae. Fossils of these simple algae have been found which are millions of years old. There are living ones in Shark Bay, Australia, where conditions haven't changed much in that time.

Normally, environments do change – though it may take a long time. Organisms may take millions of years to evolve, but if they cannot keep on adapting they die out (become extinct) if their environment changes. Natural selection has no favourites.

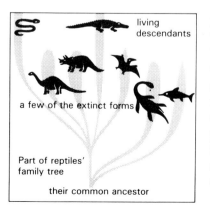

living descendants

a few of the extinct forms

Part of reptiles' family tree

their common ancestor

Darwin used the term 'natural selection' because he knew about 'artificial selection' where man selects the next generation to breed 'better' pigeons or whatever. He saw a connection with what happens in the natural world where the selective force is something like weather or predators like the owl. There were many objections to his ideas because they meant that the pattern of changes in living things was the result of chance and the physical laws of nature – that there was no plan in nature and that man was not special but an animal like others. Some people still do not accept the ideas of evolution, but today there is more evidence for it than there was in Darwin's time.

# Evolution- the evidence

The theory of evolution suggests that living organisms are descended from a common ancestor.

There is quite a lot of evidence for this. You might expect related organisms to show similarities inherited from their common ancestors – and they do.

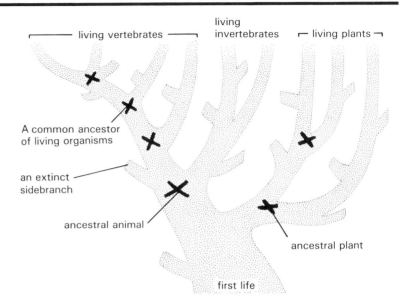

1. **Similar body plans**
   For example, vertebrate leg bones are based on the same pattern, though it is adapted for different situations in different animals.

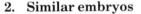
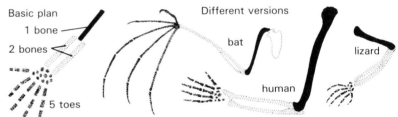

2. **Similar embryos**
   It is often hard to tell which vertebrate embryo is which when they are very young. As they grow, differences appear.

| 1 | in water | in shelled egg | in uterus |
|---|----------|----------------|-----------|
| 2 | | | |
| 3 | | | |
| | fish | tortoise | human being |

3. **Similar chemistry**
   Related organisms have inherited similar proteins. Unrelated organisms have rather different proteins, even if they look alike.

Egg white proteins show that the bustard and the seriema are related.

The secretary bird is not.

**Fossils** are the remains of long-dead organisms. They include the ancestors of living organisms. You might expect to find fossils of organisms whose descendents are different because of natural selection. These should include common ancestors of animals that are rather different from each other today. We do find such fossils, but there are big gaps. Perhaps this is not surprising. Most dead organisms rot away completely. Few of them are preserved – most are lost. Evolutionary change, when it happens, may be fairly rapid. Few organisms from 'in between' stages are fossilized. We can, however, follow the evolution of some animals – including some monkeys and a sea urchin.

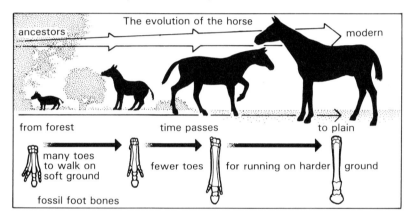

The evolution of the horse

ancestors — modern

from forest — time passes — to plain

many toes to walk on soft ground → fewer toes → for running on harder ground

fossil foot bones

You might also expect to **see evolutionary changes happening** – though only small ones, because evolution takes a long time compared to our life span. Here is one example.

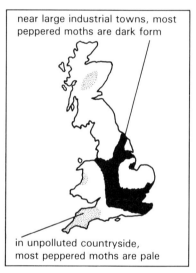

near large industrial towns, most peppered moths are dark form

in unpolluted countryside, most peppered moths are pale

There was a time when **peppered moths** in England were mostly pale. The pale ones were hard for birds to see against tree trunks covered in lichen. The dark ones were not hidden, and were mostly eaten by birds.

After the Industrial Revolution, the trees in towns had dark sooty trunks. The pale moths were easy to see on these trees, so they were eaten. In towns, the dark (melanic) form of peppered moth increased in numbers.

The map shows where the two forms of peppered moth are now found. Since the fifties, when the Clean Air Act was passed, there has been less air pollution in some areas, and lichen has been able to grow on trees again. In these areas, the melanic moths are becoming fewer compared to the pale form.

The moth population has changed in the last 100 years, because of changes in the environment.

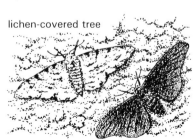

lichen-covered tree

blackened trunk

# Some evolutionary explanations

The theory of evolution helps explain some puzzling facts.

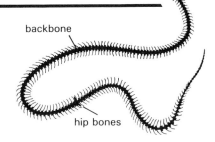

backbone

hip bones

## Vestigial organs

These are organs with no obvious use. 'Hip' bones in snakes seem pointless since snakes have no legs. But if snakes evolved from four-footed ancestors, these traces of their heritage make sense.

## Faulty genes staying in a population

Sickle-cell anaemia is an example. A surprising number of people carry this gene – up to a fifth of the population in some parts of Africa. Why? It seems to be a harmful gene and it should disappear as the result of natural selection. It turns out that people with one sickle-cell gene are less likely to suffer from malaria than people with normal red blood cells. The advantage is great enough to keep the gene going – even though children who inherit two sickle-cell genes are likely to die young.

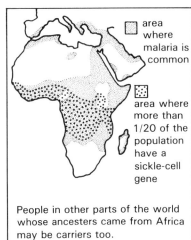

area where malaria is common

area where more than 1/20 of the population have a sickle-cell gene

People in other parts of the world whose ancesters came from Africa may be carriers too.

## Life forms on islands

These are often unusual, and fit in well with the theory. The Galapagos finches were a great puzzle for Darwin without an evolutionary explanation. The story is probably this – a pair of finches were blown to one of the islands from the South American mainland.

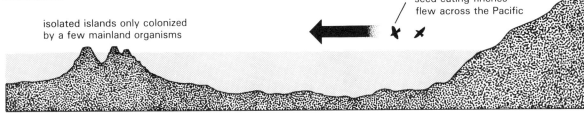

isolated islands only colonized by a few mainland organisms

ancestral seed-eating finches flew across the Pacific

On the island there was less competition than on the mainland. The descendants of the first pair evolved differently from mainland finches. They changed so that they could make use of the food available – fruit and insects as well as seeds. Some flew to other islands where conditions were slightly different and more types of finch developed.

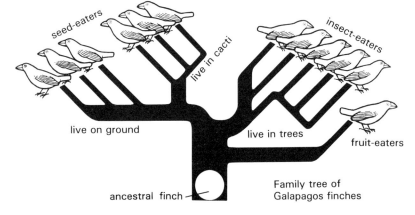

seed-eaters

live in cacti

insect-eaters

live on ground

live in trees

fruit-eaters

ancestral finch

Family tree of Galapagos finches

# Summary and questions

## Summary

Life on earth has evolved or changed over millions of years from simple organisms. Most organisms die before they reproduce. Those with adaptations which help them survive and find a mate are more likely to have offspring, and the offspring may inherit these adaptations. This is natural selection. If the environment changes, organisms which happen to be adapted to the new conditions will be the ones to survive and to breed. There is evidence from fossils, from the embryos and structure of living organisms, and (on a small scale) from examples of evolution happening over the last 100 years.

## Questions

1. Copy out and fill in the blanks.
   _____ worked for many years on his theory of evolution, in which he tried to explain how organisms _____. He said that huge numbers of organisms are born and most _____. Because organisms _____, some are better able to fight for _____ or hide from _____, and so on, than others. They are likely to have more _____ and the result is that a group of organisms gradually _____ as their _____ changes. A modern example is the _____ _____ which once was _____, and lived on light _____ covered trees. Pollution means that town trees have _____ trunks and in towns today a _____ form of the _____ is common. Selection is by _____ who eat animals they can see easily on the tree trunks.

2. (a) Humans have an appendix – a small bulge from the wall of the large intestine. It does not seem to have a use, and if it becomes infected it can make people very ill. How do you explain the fact that we have an appendix?

   (b) Mauritius is an island in the Indian Ocean far away from the mainland of Africa. On it evolved a very strange bird. It was large, moved slowly and could not fly. When man came to the island and brought mainland animals it soon became extinct. How do you explain the dodo's story – how could it evolve in the first place and why did it disappear so fast?

3. Imagine you are a reporter. You have interviewed Charles Darwin and asked him about his theory – especially where he got his ideas from. Write a short article called 'Great Naturalist Says Young People Should Travel'.

4. In this book, the theory of evolution is illustrated by mice. Explain how the theory works using another organism to illustrate each point.

5. Bacteria are normally killed by antibiotics like penicillin. Chance mutations in some bacteria make them completely or partly resistant to certain antibiotics. If a group of bacteria is exposed to an antibiotic, the resistant forms may survive and breed while the non-resistant forms die.

   (a) Make up an experiment which would show whether a sample of bacteria included any resistant forms.

   (b) Anna and Kay are ill and are given a course of penicillin tablets to take (say for a week). Anna takes all of hers but Kay only takes half, because she feels fine after a couple of days and can't be bothered. Which girl is more likely to be carrying bacteria which she could pass on to someone else? Why?

6. Write a discussion between two people – one who believes in Darwin's theory and one who does not. Include evidence for evolution, an example which it is hard to explain and something about time.

# The making of the Homo sapiens

Homo sapiens – us – has been around for a tiny fraction of the time that there has been life on Earth. The earliest fossils come from about 3 thousand million years ago, so life must have begun before that. Humanoids related to man were around 3 million years ago. That's less than a thousandth of the time we know there has been life on Earth.

We have fossil clues which give us the broad outline of the story of our evolution.

Each dot is a place where important human fossils have been found.

Cro-magnon

early man-types in Africa

The earliest ancestor we know of is a small ape type called Ramapithecus who lived 15 million years ago. All we have is bits of jaw but they are clearly more like us than modern apes.

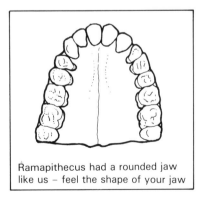

Ramapithecus had a rounded jaw like us – feel the shape of your jaw

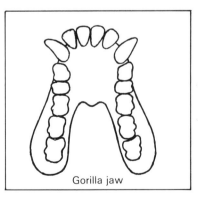

Gorilla jaw

an Australopithecine

Some of Ramapithecus' descendents evolved into the Australopithecines around 4 million years ago. They were two types – stocky five-footers and slimmer four-footers. They stood upright but probably waddled when they ran.

Between 2 and 3 million years ago, Homo habilis (handyman) joined the Australopithecines on the African plains. These people had larger brains and made simple tools.

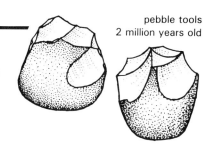

pebble tools
2 million years old

Homo erectus (upright man), who followed, was more of a traveller. Fossils of these people appear in Africa, Asia and Europe. They made more complex stone tools and used fire for cooking.

Homo erectus

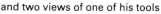

and two views of one of his tools

The Neanderthal people had brains as big as ours, but they shared heavy brows and a lack of chin with Homo erectus. Neanderthals cared about the dead. The bones of a Neanderthal child have been found surrounded by animal horns in a specially dug pit.

In one group, not only brain size but also skull shape was changing. People very like modern man were around in Europe 100 000 years ago – Homo sapiens (wise man!) had arrived.

By 25 000 years ago, people like those at Cro-magnon in France were doing well enough to have time for cave painting, carving small statues and burying their dead with care. Changes in people since then have been less biological and more social. Ideas have been passed on as people talk and write. Over the years knowledge has grown and its use has changed the way we live.

fertility goddess

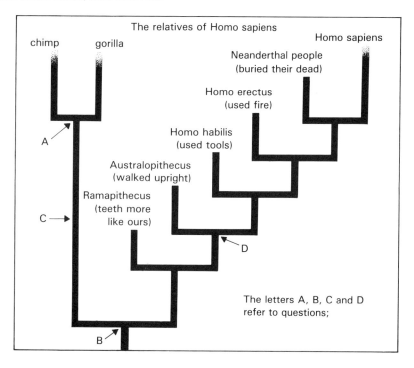

The relatives of Homo sapiens

chimp    gorilla

Homo sapiens

Neanderthal people (buried their dead)

Homo erectus (used fire)

Homo habilis (used tools)

Australopithecus (walked upright)

Ramapithecus (teeth more like ours)

A

C

D

B

The letters A, B, C and D refer to questions;

# Classification

The end results of evolution are millions of living things in thousands of breeding groups or species (more about species over the page). Species are given names – mainly so that we can talk about them to each other. Putting species into groups of various sizes makes it easier to look at relationships and to understand how bodies work. This is known as **classification**.

**Living things checklist**
Living organisms all
1. respire
2. grow
3. feed (this includes making their own food)
4. respond to stimuli
5. excrete (get rid of) wastes
6. move
7. reproduce

OUCH!

A crystal grows in a concentrated salt solution – is it alive? No, because it does none of the other things on the list.

## Naming species

Common names won't do. A robin, for example, is not the same bird in Europe and in the United States – or in Australia for that matter. A Swedish biologist called Carl Linnaeus devised a system of scientific names. Scientific names come in two parts – the **generic** name (which genus it is) and the **specific** name (which species it is). A genus is a group of closely related species.

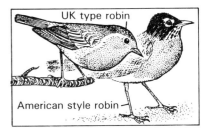
UK type robin
American style robin

Organisms with the same generic name but different specific names are closely related but cannot breed successfully. Only man has the generic name Homo, but in the past there have been at least two other related species.

**Homo** (genus bit)
**sapiens** (species bit)

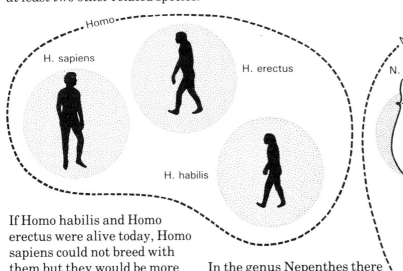
Homo
H. sapiens
H. erectus
H. habilis

If Homo habilis and Homo erectus were alive today, Homo sapiens could not breed with them but they would be more like us than, say, chimps are. Chimps have a different generic name.

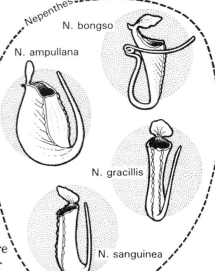
Nepenthes
N. bongso
N. ampullana
N. gracillis
N. sanguinea

In the genus Nepenthes there are several species of pitcher plants (insect-eating plants). Here are just four.

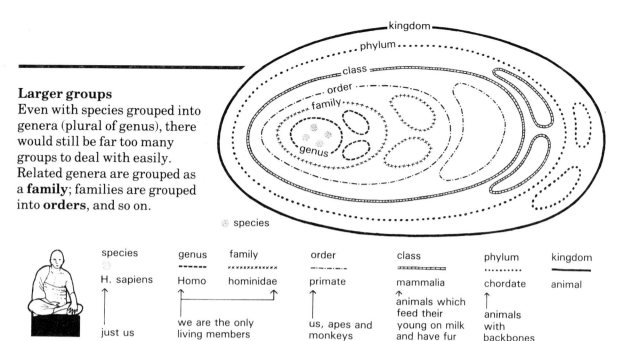

## Larger groups

Even with species grouped into genera (plural of genus), there would still be far too many groups to deal with easily. Related genera are grouped as a **family**; families are grouped into **orders**, and so on.

species

| | species | genus | family | order | class | phylum | kingdom |
|---|---|---|---|---|---|---|---|
| | H. sapiens | Homo | hominidae | primate | mammalia | chordate | animal |
| | ↑ just us | ↑ we are the only living members | | ↑ us, apes and monkeys | ↑ animals which feed their young on milk and have fur | ↑ animals with backbones | |

We classify organisms by their similarities. The greater the number of similarities two organisms have, the smaller the group they can be put into. In larger groups the similarities become fewer and more basic. Backbones came before feeding the young on milk – they are more fundamental.

bluebell
Yorkshire fog grass
poppy
A
D
E
C
fern
dandelion
wheat
B
F

B
A D F
C E

All six are plants, and all are green plants. How are we to group them? What characteristics count? Based on whether they have flowers, and the type of leaf veining, we get the boxed result.
D and F are more closely related (have more similarities) to each other than they are to A or any of the others.

The largest groups are the **kingdoms**.

After the next summary, we look at the major groups (**phyla**) in these kingdoms.

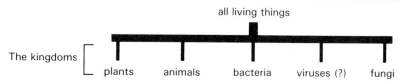

all living things

The kingdoms

plants   animals   bacteria   viruses (?)   fungi

# Species

The word 'species' comes up often in biology. It is used to describe organisms which are related closely enough to breed successfully.

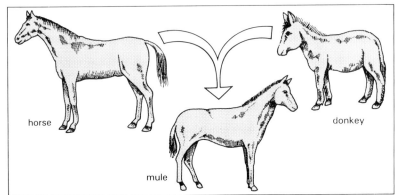

'Successfully' means that the offspring must be fertile (able to reproduce themselves). All humans belong to one fertile group – one species.

Horses and donkeys can have offspring – mules. But mules are sterile – the line stops there. So horses and donkeys are separate species.

horse

donkey

mule

During evolution new species are formed. There are several possible ways this can happen. One is isolation. One group gets divided into two by something like water. The two groups are in slightly different conditions and evolve differently. Eventually they are so different that if they happen to meet again they cannot breed – they are two species, not one. This is probably what happened to the animals on the Galapagos. Water is not the only barrier.

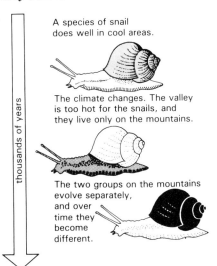

A species of snail does well in cool areas.

The climate changes. The valley is too hot for the snails, and they live only on the mountains.

The two groups on the mountains evolve separately, and over time they become different.

thousands of years

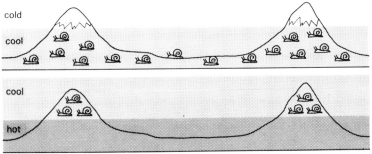

cold

cool

cool

hot

The climate changes again. The two groups can mix but are now too different to breed – they are two new species.

cold

cool

# Summary and questions

## Summary

We are beginning to understand the story of the evolution of life on earth. The end result of evolution is a wide variety of life, which we divide into groups for convenience. This is called classifying. The smallest groups are breeding groups – species. The next section summarizes the main groups in which species are arranged.

## Questions

1. This is a cartoon borrowed from a science magazine. How do you explain it?

2. On the diagram of man's family tree (page 137) there are letters A–D.
   (a) One of these represents a common ancestor shared by man and modern apes – which?
   (b) Which letter represents the common ancestor for modern man and the Australopithecines?
   (c) On the map showing where human type fossils have been found there are big gaps where none have been found. How do you explain the gaps?

3. Africa is sometimes called 'the cradle of mankind'. Why do you think this name is given? Do you think it is an accurate description?

4. Explain what is meant by
   (a) species
   (b) extinct

5. Choose **one** of these ancestors or near-ancestors of man and explain how it differed from (a) its own ancestors and (b) us: Homo habilis, Homo erectus, Australopithecus.

6. If you were given a small group (say six) of animals or plants how would you decide whether they all belonged to the same species or not? Give as many details of what you would do as you can.

7. Here are some invented animals. They belong to different species, but are all members of the order Mugwumpida. Group the species into genera and give them scientific names. Group the genera into families. You can have a genus or a family with only one species in it if you want. Give your reasons for the way you have grouped them.

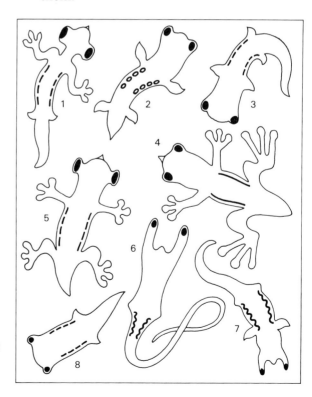

# Bacteria and viruses

## Bacteria

Bacteria are found everywhere – they are small and tough.

A bacterial cell has no nucleus (a membrane bag containing chromosomes).

Bacteria vary in shape and size.

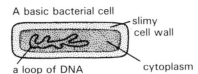

A basic bacterial cell
- slimy
- cell wall
- a loop of DNA
- cytoplasm

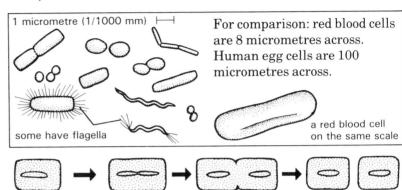

1 micrometre (1/1000 mm)

some have flagella

For comparison: red blood cells are 8 micrometres across. Human egg cells are 100 micrometres across.

a red blood cell on the same scale

Bacteria reproduce rapidly – usually by splitting in two.

Their numbers are enormous. It has been suggested that the mass of all the bacteria is 20 times that of all animal life – and that 1 gram of dead skin cells from your head contains 500 million bacteria. They have been found 6 miles down in the ocean, in hot springs at near-boiling temperatures, and floating high in the atmosphere – as well as on and in plants, animals and soil. Some bacteria feed off other organisms, alive or dead. Others make their own food using light or chemical energy.

## Helpful bacteria

Most animals cannot digest cellulose. Bacteria live in the guts of cows, horses, rabbits and so on, and break down cellulose for them.

Bacteria help in the breakdown of dead organisms – vital for the recycling of materials. We use them in sewage farms.

Bacteria in the roots of clover (and its relatives) help fix nitrogen – needed for proteins and DNA.

Cheese, butter and vinegar are the result of bacterial action. We use them to make vitamins. In the future, perhaps, we may be able to use bacteria to make insulin for diabetics, and other useful chemicals.

## Harmful bacteria

Some bacteria damage tissues or make poisons (toxins). They are the exceptions.

Bacterial diseases include gonorrhoea, whooping cough, diphtheria, tetanus (lockjaw), leprosy, and typhoid. Vaccines may help to overcome harmful bacteria, and so do antibiotics.

## Viruses

Viruses are even smaller than bacteria. They can only 'live' inside cells.

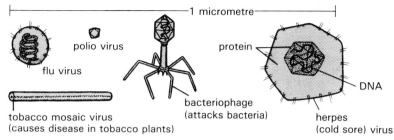

polio virus

flu virus

tobacco mosaic virus
(causes disease in tobacco plants)

bacteriophage
(attacks bacteria)

protein

DNA

herpes
(cold sore) virus

Viruses are just a length of genetic material (DNA and RNA) and one or more kinds of protein. They hardly count as life. They do not feed, breathe, grow or move – on their own they do nothing.

However, once they are inside a living cell they take over its machinery and redirect it. Instead of making more cell materials, viruses are produced. The cell eventually bursts and viruses are released to start invading cells all over again.

### A few virus diseases

polio
flu
colds
smallpox and chickenpox
measles and german measles*
mumps

*can damage unborn children.

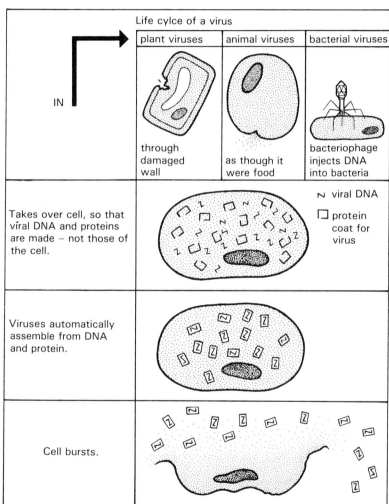

Life cylce of a virus

| | plant viruses | animal viruses | bacterial viruses |
|---|---|---|---|
| IN | through damaged wall | as though it were food | bacteriophage injects DNA into bacteria |
| Takes over cell, so that viral DNA and proteins are made – not those of the cell. | | | viral DNA, protein coat for virus |
| Viruses automatically assemble from DNA and protein. | | | |
| Cell bursts. | | | |

Viruses are parasites and can do a lot of damage. Vaccines help, provided they are used in advance, but antibiotics don't. The body's natural defence chemical, interferon, is normally produced in tiny quantities, but genetic engineering may soon mean that we can make and test interferon in large amounts.

# Fungi

Like an iceberg, most of a fungus is below the surface. Its thread-like hyphae weave through the tissues of other organisms, alive or dead, and digest them. Fungi evolved separately from green plants. As they have no chlorophyll, they cannot make their own food. Many are decomposers and, along with bacteria, are mainly responsible for recycling materials. They include yeasts and moulds as well as the mushrooms and toadstools.

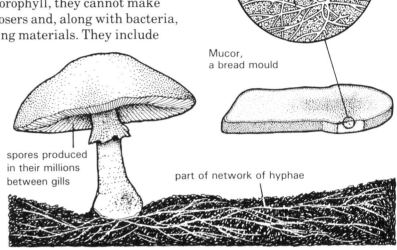

Mucor, a bread mould

Fungi produce spores, sexually or asexually, in enormous quantities. Fungal groups are identified by the way they produce spores. Mushrooms are typical of a group different from the moulds. They produce spores between the gills under the mushroom 'cap'.

spores produced in their millions between gills

part of network of hyphae

Some fungi have symbiotic relationships with other organisms. One result is a lichen – a combination of an alga and a fungus.

---

**Helpful fungi**

Decomposers recycle material.

Some are edible, e.g. field mushrooms.

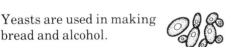

Yeasts are used in making bread and alcohol.

Many fungi produce antibiotics, e.g. penicillin (discovered by Alexander Fleming).

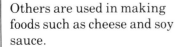

Others are used in making foods such as cheese and soy sauce.

**Harmful fungi**

Some are poisonous, e.g. death cap.

Some – not as many as bacteria and viruses – cause disease in people, e.g. athletes foot and thrush.

More cause disease in organisms useful to people, e.g. potato blight (damaged leaves mean a ruined crop),

and the smuts and rusts, which cause enormous crop losses.

# Green plants

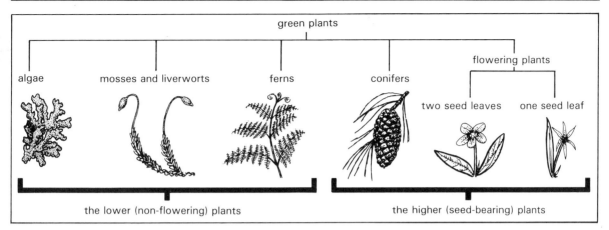

green plants

algae | mosses and liverworts | ferns | conifers | flowering plants

two seed leaves | one seed leaf

the lower (non-flowering) plants

the higher (seed-bearing) plants

## Algae
Algae are a mixed bunch –
everything from single-celled
organisms to huge seaweeds.

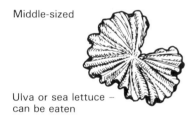

Middle-sized

Ulva or sea lettuce –
can be eaten

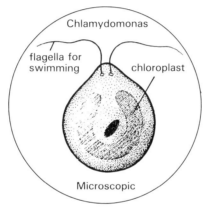

Chlamydomonas

flagella for
swimming

chloroplast

Microscopic

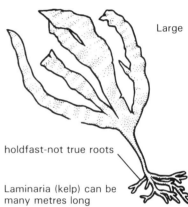

Large

holdfast-not true roots

Laminaria (kelp) can be
many metres long

All algae have chlorophyll and can make their own food. Some
groups have other pigments which mask the green of chlorophyll,
and so they may look brown or red.

Their structure is simple. Large algae – lacking support – must
live in the water. Many small algae float in the surface waters as
part of the plankton, while others are found in soil or growing on
buildings and trees. Look for pleurococcus on the shady side of
trees. It's a green powdery alga.

Pleurococcus

Seaweeds are used as manure and as food – especially in Japan.
Agar – the jelly bacteria are often grown on – is made from
seaweed. Seaweed jellys are used in making beer, cosmetics,
paint, ice cream, film and many other things.

capsules for pills

# More green plants

## Mosses

Mosses and their relatives are the next step for plant life. They live on land, but most prefer damp, shady places to live. They produce spores in a spore capsule, and their 'leaves' and 'roots' are simpler than those of higher plants.

There is a sexual stage in the production of the spore capsule, but the spores are asexual. The plant does not have special cells for transporting food and water, and there are no support tissues – mosses remain small.

Important mosses include sphagnum moss, which is involved in colonizing open water and turning it first into a peat bog and then into dry land able to support trees. Peat is used as fuel in some places.

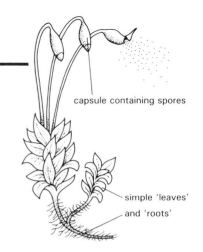

capsule containing spores

simple 'leaves' and 'roots'

sphagnum

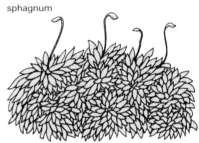

Mosses help prevent soil erosion, and also break down rocks.

## Ferns

Ferns are better adapted to life on land than mosses. They have a transport system and stiffened support in their stems. It is simple, but it allows ferns to grow large.

They still need water for part of their life cycle.

tree fern from Australia

The adult plant grows from an egg cell fertilized by a sperm which swims towards it through a water film. You could say that ferns still have one foot in the water.

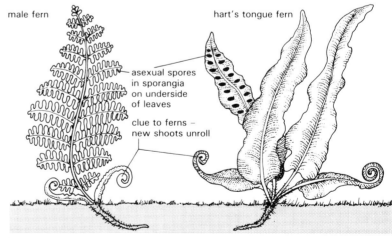

male fern

hart's tongue fern

asexual spores in sporangia on underside of leaves

clue to ferns – new shoots unroll

Most ferns are looked on as attractive and many are grown in gardens and greenhouses. Bracken, on the other hand, counts as a weed – it grows very well on land that could be used for pasture.

## Conifers

Conifers can grow very successfully on dry land, thanks to an improved plumbing system, and to pollen. Instead of sperm which swim, they have a waterproof male gamete to fertilize egg cells on the scales of female cones. The resulting seeds fall out when the cone opens. (They have no protective coatings as there's no ovary to make them.)

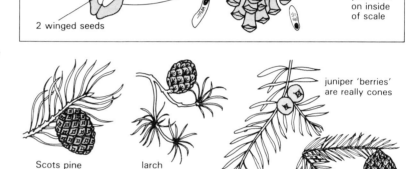

cone scale
embryo
2 winged seeds
pollen from male cone
egg cells produced on inside of scale

Conifers were fully developed 220 million years ago. Today the group includes firs, pines and yews. Among them are the bristle cone pines, thought to be the oldest living plants on earth. One is believed to be 5000 years old.

Leaf patterns and cone shapes help identify conifers.

Scots pine
larch
juniper 'berries' are really cones
Norway spruce (Christmas tree)

## Flowering plants

Equipped with adaptable leaves, effective transport systems, flowers and double-wrapped seeds, flowering plants have beaten conifers into second place as land plants. They come in two groups, depending on whether they have one seed leaf or two.

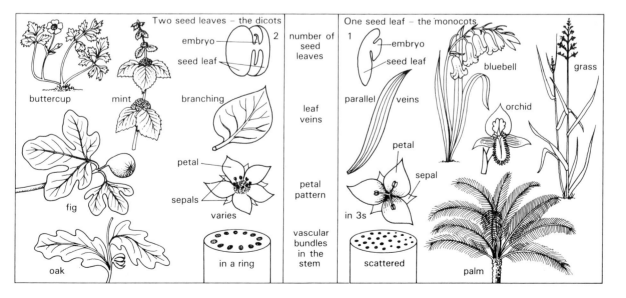

Two seed leaves – the dicots
embryo
seed leaf
2
number of seed leaves
1
One seed leaf – the monocots
embryo
seed leaf
bluebell
grass
buttercup
mint
branching
leaf veins
parallel veins
orchid
petal
sepals
varies
petal
petal pattern
in 3s
petal
sepal
fig
vascular bundles in the stem
oak
in a ring
scattered
palm

147

# The animal kingdom

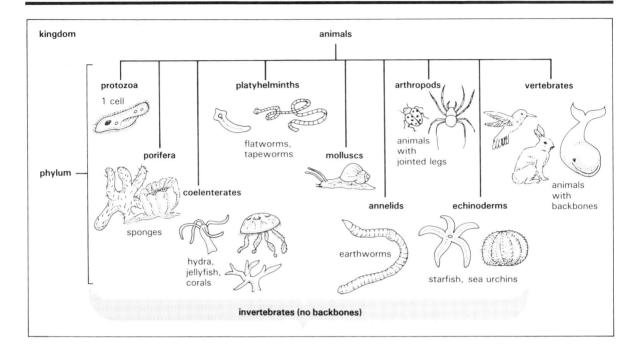

The major groups of invertebrates are as different from each other as they are from vertebrates. They make up 95 per cent of all animal species. The diagram above leaves out the smaller of the twenty-five phyla of invertebrates.

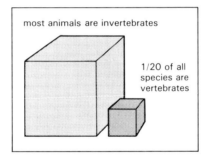

most animals are invertebrates

1/20 of all species are vertebrates

## Protozoa – the single-celled animals

Some classifiers would like to put all single-celled organisms in one group – the protists. There are not only animal-type and plant-type single-celled organisms, but also some which show features of both. Chlamydomonas, for example, may be described as an alga in one book and be included as a protist in a book on animals. Decide for yourself whether it matters.
Protozoa include Amoeba, Paramecium and Plasmodium.

Protozoa all need water to survive, though some can live through dry times in waterproof cysts. They may be free-living like Amoeba (found in ponds) or live on or in other organisms. Plasmodium is a parasite which causes malaria. Other protozoan diseases include a form of dysentry, and sleeping sickness.

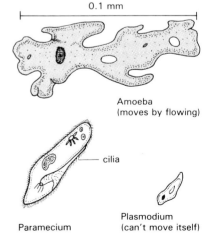

0.1 mm

Amoeba
(moves by flowing)

cilia

Paramecium

Plasmodium
(can't move itself)

148

## Sponges (Porifera)

A bath sponge is just a skeleton – in life it is completely covered with a layer of loosely organized cells. Sponges lie anchored to the sea floor (or a few in fresh water). They have a variety of cell types, including some with flagella. These beat and keep water moving through the animal. Food particles in the water are trapped and digested.

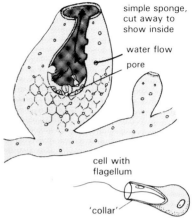

simple sponge, cut away to show inside

water flow

pore

cell with flagellum

Other cells make the skeleton of the sponge. In bath sponges this is mainly a protein called spongin (yes, really!), but in others the skeleton is reinforced by 'needles' of calcium carbonate or, in the glass sponges, silica.

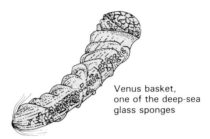

Venus basket, one of the deep-sea glass sponges

'collar'

Sponges reproduce sexually and asexually.

## Coelenterates

These include animals whose bodies are based on two layers of cells which work together as a whole.

They have tentacles with stinging cells to paralyse their prey. The tentacles, working together, push the food into the mouth. Digestion is inside the body tube. Coelenterates can all move, or at least move their tentacles, and many can glide or swim. Reproduction is sexual or asexual.

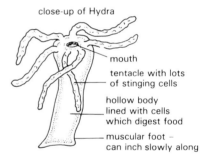

close-up of Hydra

mouth

tentacle with lots of stinging cells

hollow body lined with cells which digest food

muscular foot – can inch slowly along

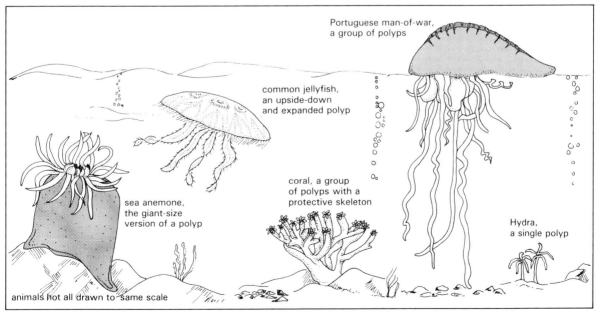

Portuguese man-of-war, a group of polyps

common jellyfish, an upside-down and expanded polyp

coral, a group of polyps with a protective skeleton

sea anemone, the giant-size version of a polyp

Hydra, a single polyp

animals not all drawn to same scale

149

# More invertebrates

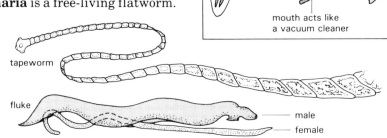

position of gut.
No blood system

mouth acts like
a vacuum cleaner

### Platyhelminths – flatworms

These are simple animals with a body plan which is bilaterally symmetrical. That is, one half is a mirror image of the other, on a line drawn from head to tail. **Planaria** is a free-living flatworm.

Other flatworms do more damage – they include parasites like tapeworms, found in guts, and flukes.

tapeworm

The blood fluke Schistosoma harms 200 million people.

fluke

male

female

### Annelids – segmented worms

These have bodies which are divided into similar sections, with a gut and nerve cord and blood vessels running through it.

They include earthworms

and rag worms (which live in mud by the sea)

as well as blood-sucking parasites – the leeches.

### Molluscs

The basic mollusc plan is a soft body full of guts, reproductive organs and so on, covered by a mantle – a sheet of tissue which sometimes produces a shell. They include snails, slugs, bivalves (which have two shells), octopuses and squids.

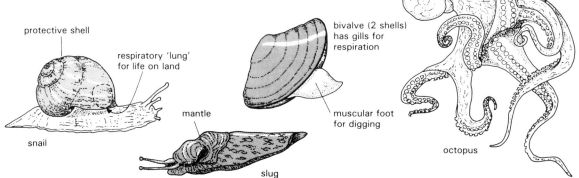

protective shell

respiratory 'lung'
for life on land

snail

mantle

slug

bivalve (2 shells)
has gills for
respiration

muscular foot
for digging

octopus

## Arthropods

These animals with their jointed legs form a huge group. They have a tough exoskeleton, which covers a body which is often in segments. The arthropods show adaptations for many ways of life which include life

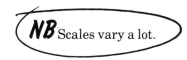

### in the water

### on land

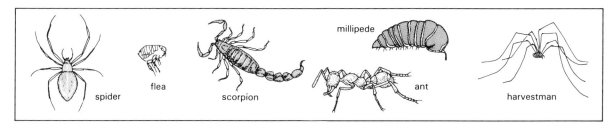

### and in the air

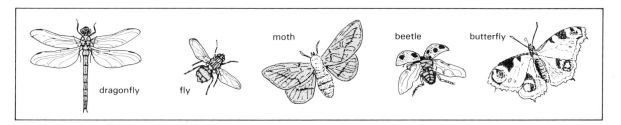

and so on for thousands of species.

## Echinoderms

These have bodies which divide into five equal sections, not two. They move slowly – lacking head or brain – on tube feet powered by hydraulic (water) pressure. Chalky plates under the skin provide protection for starfish.

Roll up a starfish into a ball, add spines and you have a sea urchin.

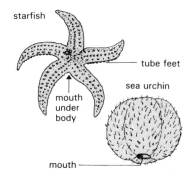

# Animals with backbones

The vertebrates, with their brains and spinal cords protected by skull and vertebrae, have done well. These two pages are a reminder of the groups that make up the phylum (phyla is the plural).

## Fish

Fish live in water, are cold-blooded and, mainly, breathe through gills. Their muscular, scale-clad bodies are built around two types of skeleton – cartilage and bone.

The bony fish have evolved many forms, from eel-shape to plate-shape and to flying fins.

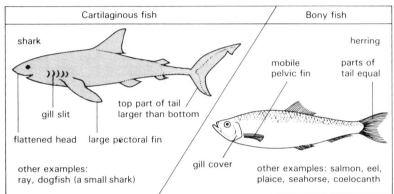

Cartilaginous fish

shark

gill slit

flattened head    large pectoral fin

top part of tail larger than bottom

other examples:
ray, dogfish (a small shark)

Bony fish

herring

mobile pelvic fin    parts of tail equal

gill cover

other examples: salmon, eel, plaice, seahorse, coelocanth

## Amphibians

The first of the land-living vertebrates, most amphibians have a thin scale-less skin and must remain in a damp environment or die from dehydration. Their young are tadpoles living in water and breathing through gills, but the adults have lungs. They include salamanders and newts, as well as toads and frogs (tail-less as adults).

## Reptiles

Reptiles are more adapted for life on land. They are cold-blooded, with thick scaly skins. They lay eggs with leathery shells from which mini-adults emerge already breathing with lungs. They include turtles and tortoises, lizards, snakes and crocodilians.

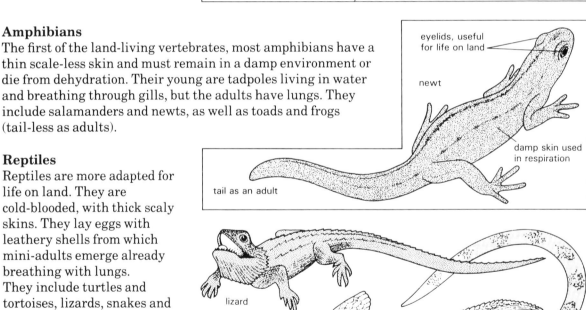

eyelids, useful for life on land

newt

damp skin used in respiration

tail as an adult

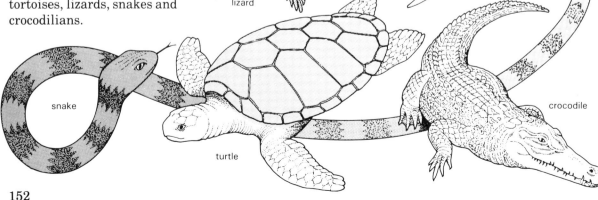

lizard

snake

turtle

crocodile

## Birds

Very early fossil birds are hard to tell from the fossils of some dinosaurs – and it seems likely that birds are descended from early reptiles. Scales have become feathers. Birds are warm-blooded – that is, they have a steady body temperature and a four-chambered heart. They have no teeth. They range from flightless kiwis to birds of paradise, with a lot of variety in between.

bird of paradise

## Mammals

Mammals started in a small way at the beginning of the age of dinosaurs. They have fur and feed their young on milk from mammary glands. They are warm-blooded and generally have large brains.

kiwi

**Monotremes** include the platypus and the spiny anteater. They lay eggs but feed their young on milk.

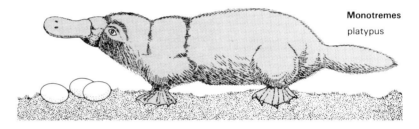

Monotremes

platypus

**Marsupials** include kangaroos. The young start life inside the mother, but there is no placenta, so they are born at an early stage of development and grow in the mother's pouch.

Marsupials

kangaroo

**Placentals** have young which are born well developed, thanks to the placenta.

Placentals

bat

and so on

dolphin     hippo

153

# CSE examination questions

1. In an American city, garbage disposal units (machines which grind up household refuse to a sludge) became very popular. The sludge they made was passed into the sewage system and provided food for rats. In the same city, alligators were popular as pets, but some escaped or were carelessly put into the sewage system.
   (a) In this food chain state:
       (i) the producer
       (ii) the primary consumers
       (iii) the secondary consumers
   (b) State what you would expect to happen to the population of the rats before the introduction of alligators into the sewers.
   (c) If garbage disposal units were no longer to be used, state what you would expect to happen to the population of alligators in the sewers.

2. The table shows the vitamin and mineral salt content of some foods.
   From the choice of foods in the table:
   (a) Name **two** foods which you should eat or drink to avoid night blindness. Give a reason for your answer.
   (b) Name **two** foods which you should eat or drink to avoid rickets. Give a reason for each answer to (b).
   (c) Name **one** food which you should eat or drink to avoid anaemia. Give a reason for your answer.
   (d) Name **one** food which you should eat or drink to avoid scurvy.

3. (a) After digestion, some food materials are in the form of amino acids, glycerol and fatty acids. State how the body uses these:
       (i) animo acids
       (ii) glycerol and fatty acids
   (b) If a person takes into his body more food substances than he can use, explain what happens to the extra amounts which he does not require:
       (i) extra amino acids
       (ii) extra glucose
       (iii) extra glycerol and fatty acids

4. Complete **each** of the following statements by choosing the most suitable word or phrase from those in the brackets:
   (a) Lack of the mineral (**calcium, iron, salt, iodine, copper**) causes anaemia.
   (b) The enzyme (**amylase, pepsin, lipase, rennin**) breaks down starch to maltose.
   (c) Penicillin was discovered by (**Mendel, Harvey, Fleming, Jenner, Darwin**).
   (d) When iodine is added to a piece of potato it goes blue/black proving (**glucose, fat, water, starch, cellulose**) is present.
   (e) The energy to drive photosynthesis comes from (**glucose, oxygen, chlorophyll, sunlight, carbon dioxide**).
   (f) The most energy is given by (**carbohydrates, fats, proteins, vitamins, water**).

| Type of food | Vitamin A mg/100 g dry weight | Vitamin D mg/100 g dry weight | Vitamin C mg/100 g dry weight | Calcium mg/100 g dry weight | Iron mg/100 g dry weight |
|---|---|---|---|---|---|
| Liver | 15 000 | 0.9 | 24 | 8 | 4 |
| Oranges | 0 | 0.15 | 50 | 7 | 0 |
| Green beans | 0 | 0 | 25 | 18 | 1.6 |
| Milk | 930 | 1.2 | 2.7 | 300 | 0.5 |
| Butter | 2820 | 11.4 | 3 | 225 | 0.2 |

**5.** (a) Give **two** important features of all respiratory surfaces.

   (b) (i) Draw and label a diagram to show the structure of the respiratory organs of man or any other named mammal.

      (ii) Explain how air is drawn into the lungs. Use diagrams to illustrate your answer.

   (c) Yeast is an organism which can respire anaerobically.

      (i) Explain what this statement means.

      (ii) Name **one** important industry which makes use of the fact that yeast is able to respire in this manner.

**6.** A large number of wheat grains were germinated and samples of 50 seeds or seedlings removed from time to time. These samples were oven dried, then weighed. The results are shown in the table below.

| Age of seedling in days | 0 | 2 | 4 | 6 | 10 | 12 |
|---|---|---|---|---|---|---|
| Weight when dried (g) | 10 | 7 | 5 | 9 | 26 | 44 |

   (a) Plot a graph from these results.

   (b) Why does the dry weight decrease up to day 4?

   (c) Where does the extra weight come from between day 4 and 12?

**7.** Most of the energy used by a living thing is obtained by the oxidation of food materials such as sugar.

   (a) (i) The process of oxidation of food materials in a cell is known as _____.

      (ii) Some of the energy set free during the oxidation of food materials by living things escapes as heat. Describe an experiment to show that living things do produce heat. Include a suitable control.

   (b) Examine the following table showing the amount of energy needed by different kinds of people, depending on their age and the amount of physical work they do.

| Age in years | Males (joules per day) | Females (joules per day) |
|---|---|---|
| 11–14 | 11 000 | 11 000 |
| 15–19 | 14 000 | 10 000 |
| Over 19 resting | 7 000 | 6 000 |
| light work | 11 000 | 9 000 |
| heavy work | 14 000 | 12 000 |

      (i) How much more energy per day is required by 20-year-old males doing heavy work than 20-year-old females doing heavy work?

      (ii) Which group has the largest difference in energy needs between males and females?

**8.** (a) Describe briefly:

      (i) **three** important ways in which growth in mammals differs from plant growth.

      (ii) **two** ways in which growth in mammals resembles plant growth.

   (b) Animals often have a different form and habitat when young. Such a young animal is called a larva.

      (i) Draw and label a named larva.

      (ii) List **four** important differences in habits, diet or appearances between this larva and its adult form.

9. Describe what is meant by **four** of the following terms, giving examples from **named** habitats which you have studied and including references to **named** animal and plant examples.
   - (a) Colonization
   - (b) Succession
   - (c) Climax flora and fauna
   - (d) Food chains
   - (e) Climatic factors
   - (f) Competition

10. A gardener has crossed 50 plants with purple petals with 50 plants with white petals. In the first generation all plants had purple petals. He allowed these plants to self-pollinate. In the second generation 1000 plants grew. Some of these had purple petals and some had white petals.

   *First parents* (P)      Purple petals × White petals

   *First generation* (F1)      All purple petals

   *Second parents*      Purple petals × Purple petals

   *Second generation* (F2) White petals      Purple petals

   - (a) (i) Which colour is recessive?
     - (ii) Give a reason for your answer.
   - (b) (i) About how many purple-petalled plants would he have in the second generation?
     - (ii) About how many white-petalled plants would he have in the second generation?
   - (c) Who first discovered this pattern of inheritance?

11. (a) Describe with the aid of a fully labelled diagram, the structure of the heart.
   - (b) Show by means of arrows, the path taken by the blood through the heart.
   - (c) List any **four** functions of the heart.

12. A form of peppered moth, which is dark-coloured, lives mainly in industrial areas because it
   - **A** is a mutant.
   - **B** is a well camouflaged from its natural predators.
   - **C** tastes nasty.
   - **D** can only find food in such areas.
   - **E** can withstand a polluted atmosphere.

13. Which of the following statements best describes the function of the synovial membrane?
   - **A** Joins muscles to bones.
   - **B** Contracts to bring about movement.
   - **C** Holds bones together at a joint.
   - **D** Covers the ends of bones at a joint.
   - **E** Produces lubricating fluid.

14. Adrenalin, a substance produced by the adrenal gland,
   - **A** controls growth.
   - **B** prepares the body for rapid action in an emergency.
   - **C** stimulates secretion of the digestive juice.
   - **D** influences secondary sexual characteristics.
   - **E** reduces inflammation caused by bacteria or wounds.

15. It is possible to make glass filters which will allow some sorts of light to pass through them and block (stop) other sorts of light from passing through them.

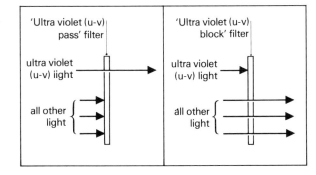

Bees frequently visit poppy flowers. Poppy petals reflect the orange-red part of light and also some of the ultra-violet radiation. Examine the diagram below showing the behaviour of such bees.

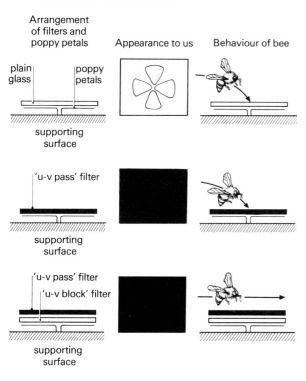

(a) From the information given in the diagram above suggest one difference between the eyes of a bee and a human.

(b) Complete the following diagram. How would the arrangement appear to us and what would be the behaviour of the bee?

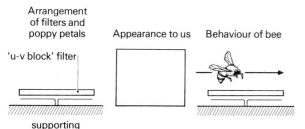

(c) (i) If a person reading a book looks up and focuses on a distant object, the lenses in his eyes undergo a change. What change takes place and how is the change brought about?

(ii) Explain fully how the human eye adjusts to the change from dim to very bright light.

16. The diagram below shows a section through a human ear.

(a) Three small bones which transmit vibrations from the eardrum to the oval window have been omitted. Complete the diagram to show these three bones and label each one of them.

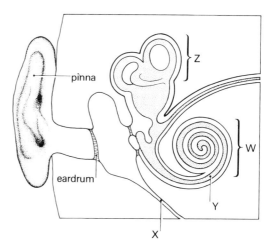

(b) State what tubes X and Y contain.

(c) State one function of
(i) W
(ii) Z

(d) Describe **two** ways in which the eardrum is protected from injury.

**17.** Fill in the gaps in the sentences. Choose your words from the list below. The same word may be used more than once.

enzymes  oxidized  parasites  reduced
symbiosis  salts  diffusion  saprophytes

The group of fungi which obtain their food substances from dead organic food materials are called _____. The complex food material has to be digested before it can get into the hyphae. This process is speeded up by the activity of chemicals known as _____. The food enters the fungus by a process known as _____ and some of it is _____ to provide energy for the growth of the fungus.

**18.** Some saliva was mixed with a little starch solution in a test-tube immersed in a water bath at 20°C. The time taken for the starch-enzyme solution to give no colour change with iodine solution was noted.
    The experiment was repeated for temperatures of 30°C, 40°C, 50°C and 60°C.

**Results**

| Temperature °C | 20 | 30 | 40 | 50 | 60 |
|---|---|---|---|---|---|
| Time taken for solution to give no colour with iodine solution (min) | | 9 | 5 | 2 | 4 | 10 |

(a) (i) What in general can be said about enzyme action in relation to temperature from these results?
    (ii) At what temperature did the enzyme act best?
(b) The normal body temperature is about 37°C. What relationship is there between this and the results?
(c) Give **two** other properties of enzymes (which are not directly related to temperature).

**19.** Look at the diagram below of part of a male urino-genital system.

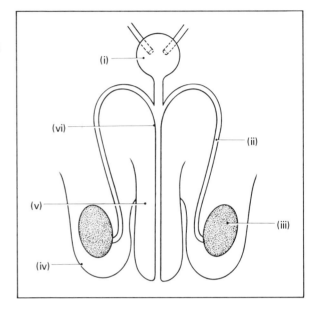

(a) Name the parts labelled (i) to (vi).
(b) Where are the sperms made?
(c) Why are the testes carried on the outside of the body?
(d) Why are so many sperms released by the male during mating?
(e) What is meant by 'puberty'?
(f) What are female reproductive cells called?
(g) Where are the female reproductive cells formed?

**20.** (a) Describe how **one** bacterium is used for man's benefit.
(b) Name **one** disease which is caused by a bacterium.
(c) Describe under the headings method, expected results and control, how you would demonstrate that bacterial spores are carried in the air.

**21.** The diagram below shows the skeleton of the arm and the muscles responsible for the raising and lowering of the arm.

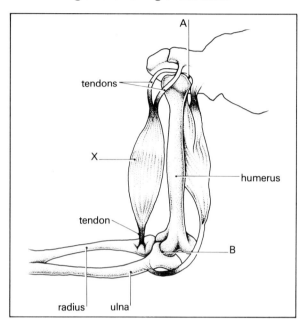

(a) Muscle X has to contract in order to raise the lower arm. What is meant when we say that a muscle has contracted?

(b) Describe how the contraction of muscle X results in the raising of the forearm.

(c) Complete the table below to show **two** differences between muscles and tendons.

| | Muscles | Tendons |
|---|---|---|
| 1. | | |
| 2. | | |

(d) Name the types of movable joint present at
   (i) A
   (ii) B

(e) (i) Draw a diagram of the internal structure of a movable joint. On your diagram label the following parts: synovial fluid, ligament, cartilage, bone.
   (ii) Explain the function of each of the following: synovial fluid, ligaments, cartilage.

(f) (i) What must happen to muscle X if the forearm is to be lowered?
   (ii) Explain why it is essential that the tendon attaching muscle X to the bone is attached to the radius rather than the humerus.

(g) If a limb bone from a small mammal is placed in dilute hydrochloric acid for several hours, the bone becomes very soft and easily bent. Explain why this so.

**22.** (a) Lizards and pigeons have scales on their legs and lay eggs. Write down **two** other ways in which they are alike.

(b) Write down **four** ways in which they are different.

(c) Explain the lifecycles of a lizard and of a pigeon in order to show how similar they are.

(d) Explain the life history of a frog so as to show how different it is from that of a lizard.

(e) Is the life cycle of the frog more suited to its own habitat (where it lives) than to the habitat of the lizard? Write down the reasons for your answer.

**23.** A balanced diet is one which
   **A** contains equal amounts of carbohydrates and proteins.
   **B** has the right quantity of all food requirements.
   **C** does not make you fat.
   **D** gives you enough energy to survive.

# Index

If you want to look something up, try the contents page first. This index gives key words which are not in the contents list.